The Complete-Blues Piano

Southern House Publishing

Copyright © 2018 Southern House Publishing

All rights reserved.
No part of this book may be reproduced in any form
by electronic, mechanical or other means
without prior permission from the publisher.

ISBN: 978-1-9997478-3-1

tylermusic.co.uk

CONTENTS

Introduction	1
Blues Styles	3 - 6
Background Theory/Info	9 - 15
Chord Progressions	16 - 25
Blues Shuffle Feel	26 - 27
Chords And Scales	28 - 89
Intervals	90 - 100
Blues Techniques	101 - 118
Boogie-Blues	121 - 179
Walking Bass	180 - 189
Slow Blues	190 - 200
Stride Piano	201 - 217
New Orleans	218 - 230
Practice Ideas	231 - 232
Downloadable Audio	233

Introduction

Welcome to 'The Complete Blues Piano' a book written to help the new blues piano player discover the blues and start their journey into this amazing style of music. The subject of blues piano is a large and varied one, especially for what appears on the surface to be a relatively simple form of music. Simple in some respects it may be, but what a wonderful form of music it is. Personally I feel that it's probably the most expressive form of music out there. Fast to slow, from emotional highs to lows, play angry, then soft, and all within just twelve bars. With the freedom to improvise and express yourself with whatever comes to mind, this ladies and gentlemen is what music is all about.

If you are reading this, then I can probably assume that you have at least some knowledge of blues music, having listened to it and most likely already played some on the piano. The purpose of this book is twofold, for one, it aims to give you enough of the theory to understand the underpinnings and so help you to be-able to improvise (and this is very much an improvisational style of music) rather than just copy and memorise from a song book (although do this also) which leaves you with little real in-depth knowledge of the music. And two, cover different styles of blues playing (as it is quite varied) from boogie-blues to slow-blues, Chicago to New Orleans, encompassing the different forms and styles of playing.

The old blues musicians of yesteryear would have learnt by ear, having had no formal means of musical education available, perhaps because of this, many people claim that 'the blues' is not something you can really learn from a book, and while I agree with this to a degree, you have to begin somewhere and having the basics written out in-front of you is worth its weight in gold. That said, there is no book anywhere on any in-depth subject that can cover everything, so learn what you can from every source you can find available, listen, read, copy, practice but most of all, just enjoy the blues.

Blues Styles

The blues first developed at around the turn of the last century, with the early recordings making it onto records around the 1920s. But there are a fair number of different styles of blues music as it had developed in several regions over a period of time. So although they have much in common, they each have a sound of their own. Here's a brief run down of a selection of the more notable styles.

Delta Blues

The Delta blues (sometimes referred to as Mississippi blues) is a style that grew up in the Delta region of the Mississippi, being from the cotton producing fields rather than the actual Mississippi River. It is traditionally more of an acoustic form, with the original recordings being from the 1920s – 1930s, with the guitar/slide guitar and harmonica being the dominant instruments used (before the use of electric guitars). Traditionally the artist often worked solo, accompanying themselves with the guitar, with elaborate finger picking styles and some slide work, all with a deep emotion that is what the blues is about.

Artists include the likes of...

Robert Johnson
Charlie Patton
Willie Brown
Son House
Bukka White

Memphis Blues

This could be referring to two different types of blues music, one from the 1920s during the tent and medicine show era. The other from the 1950s, when it plugged itself into the mains and went electric, probably making it more appealing to fans of the Chicago style. Here the style became quite heavy and aggressive with the guitars often with quite a distorted sound.

Artists include the likes of...

Furry Lewis
Gus Cannon
Memphis Willie B
Pat Hare
Joe Willie Wilkins

Texas Blues

Texas blues has been around since the early twentieth century and can be characterized by a swing influenced, relaxed and laid back feel, that is often slightly behind the beat, sometimes referred to as being the 'Texas shuffle'. Also known for its single stringed guitar solos by the likes of T-Bone Walker, who was a big influence on later blues guitarists.

Artists include the likes of...

T-Bone Walker
Blind Lemon Jefferson
Albert Collins
Lightning Hopkins
Stevie Ray Vaughan
Clarence Brown

Jump Blues

Jump blues is a style that grew out from the Boogie Woogie era, combining blues with big-band jazz influences, for a more up-tempo style, a precursor to rhythm and blues music. Consider it based around boogie-woogie with a big-band of trumpets, trombones, and saxophone players backing a lead singer, and you have the rough idea of the style. Like many forms of music, it enjoys a revival from time to time.

Artists include the likes of...

Roy Brown
Louis Jordan
Jimmy Liggins
Cab Calloway
Roy Milton
Big Joe Turner

New Orleans Blues

New Orleans blues is a style that developed around the city of New Orleans. It is heavily influenced by Caribbean rhythms, particularly the Rumba beat, along with the second-line strut. It is in a sense very much a mix of musical styles that blended so well together, creating this unique rollicking style of blues. Unlike many of the forms of blues which are far more guitar orientated, this style contains some great heavily rhythmic piano playing.

Artists include the likes of...

Professor Long Hair
Mac Rebennack
James Booker
Fats Domino
Smiley Lewis
Snooks Eaglin
Johnny Jones

Chicago Blues

Chicago blues is perhaps what the majority of people think of when they think of the 'blues', conjuring up images of musicians jamming in smoke filled blues clubs. It is very much an electric style, that developed with the migrations of workers from the south into the city back in the 1930s and 1940s. It's a bit of a hybrid, being influenced by the Delta, but pumped up with an electrified amplified sound. It is probably the single most popular and widely heard form of blues music. Instrument wise it is perhaps more varied than some styles, making use of everything, including bass, drums, guitars, vocals, harmonica, Hammond organs and of course the piano.

Artists include the likes of...

Buddy Guy
Little Walter
Muddy Waters
Junior Wells
Howlin' Wolf
Otis Spann
Memphis Slim

Modern Electric Blues

Modern electric blues is really a mix of styles, influenced by the styles of the 1950s and 1960s, predominantly Chicago, but also Texas. At times, it also combines a degree of rock and funk influences too, so some of this is very much blues in the traditional form, whereas other artists work on interesting new interpretations. Like many styles of music, there are no rules, you always have the classic original styles, but music also evolves into new territory.

Artists include the likes of...

Robert Cray
George Thorogood.
Luther Allison
Stevie Ray Vaughan
Kenny Wayne Shepherd
Joe Bonamassa

Piano Blues

Piano blues often refers to the off-shoot sub-genres of barrel-house and boogie-woogie piano that were most popular during the 1930s. These piano based styles developed before the guitar became the most dominant blues instrument. They are very closely related to the blues, but they are off-shoots and considered styles of their own. The term 'piano blues' to my mind though, really just encompasses every style of blues that's played on the piano, either solo or within a band setting, if it's blues on a piano, then it's piano blues.

Artists include the likes of...

Albert Ammons
Pete Johnson
Otis Spann
Meade Lux Lewis
Johnnie Johnson
Jimmy Yancey

Behind The Blues

A Little Theory

Major Scales

Before we delve into the blues, we will skim over some music theory as this background knowledge will help later on in the book. If you already know all of this then please feel free to move past it.

The major scale is the fundamental basis of most contemporary music and a basic knowledge of this will help you understand how the blues chord progressions work, how the chords themselves are formed and how to play in different keys.

Major Scale In 'C'

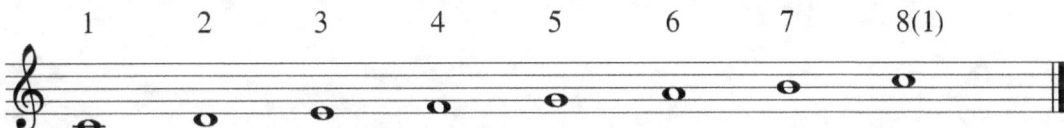

The major scale starts on the root note (in this case 'C') and moves in a set pattern of intervals until it reaches the root note again, one octave higher than it began. The pattern remains the same regardless of which key you are in. A whole step moves two semi-tones up (two keys), a half step moves one semi-tone up (one key).

Whole step, whole step, half step, whole step, whole step, whole step, half step

W-W-H-W-W-W-H

> If you can remember this pattern then it becomes easy to work out any of the major scales by simply starting on the root note and following the set pattern. All notes are referred to as being degrees of the scale, with one (the root) being the first degree and five being the fifth degree. So when someone says 'the fifth' it is the fifth degree of the scale they are referring to, in the example above this would be 'G'.

Key of A

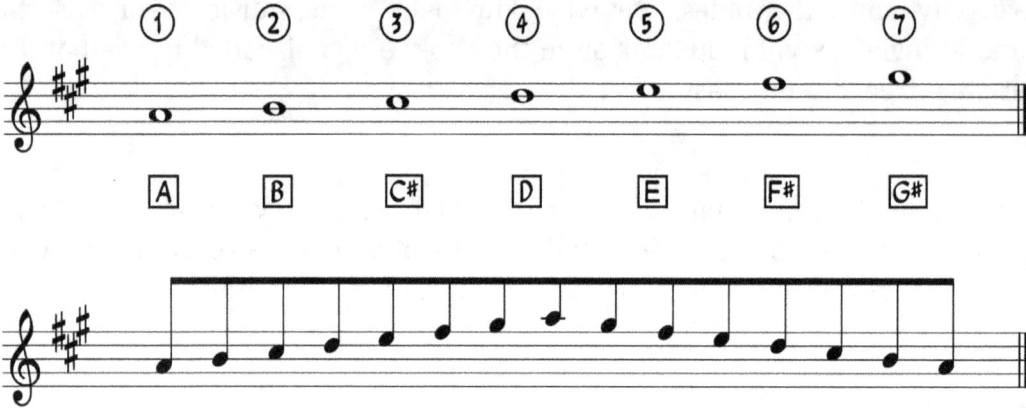

Key of B♭

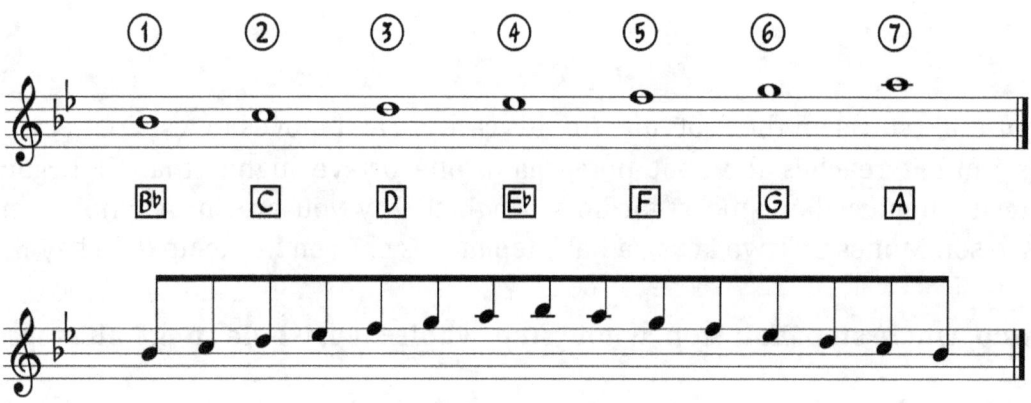

Key of B

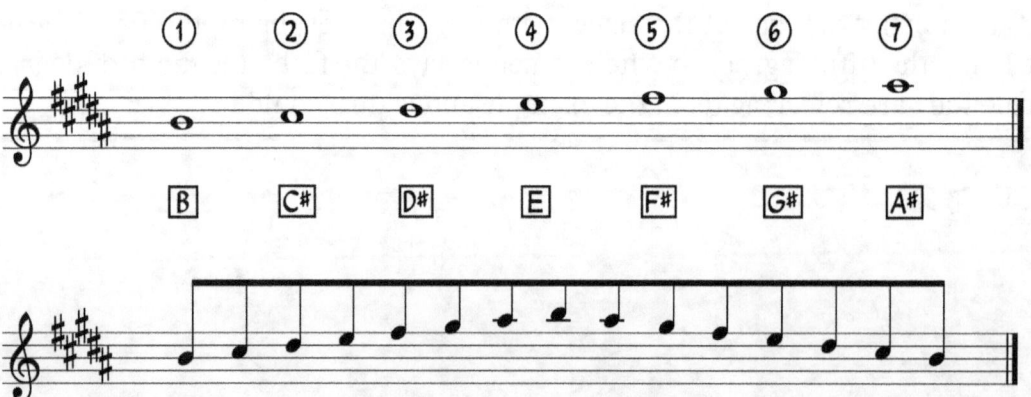

Key of C

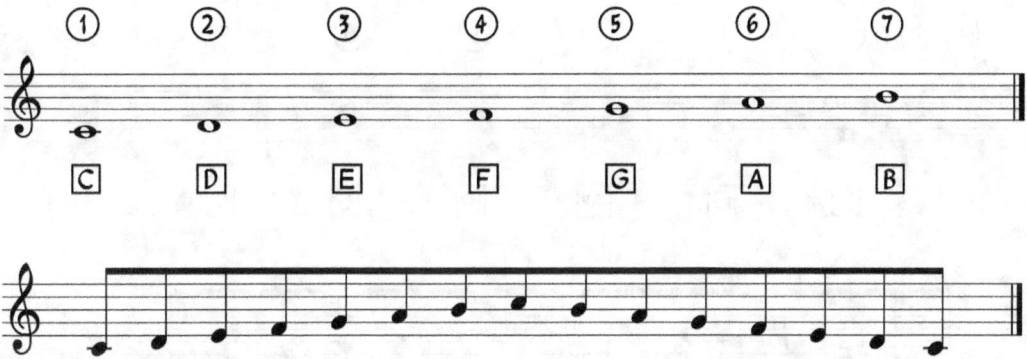

Key of D♭

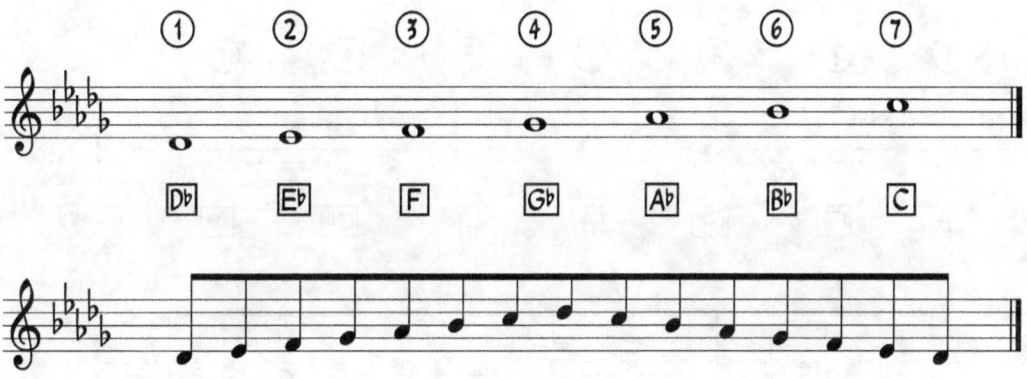

Key of D

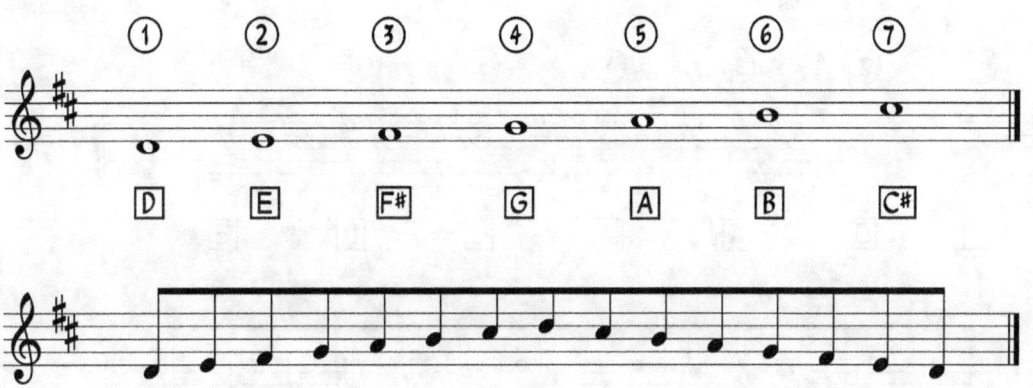

Key of E♭

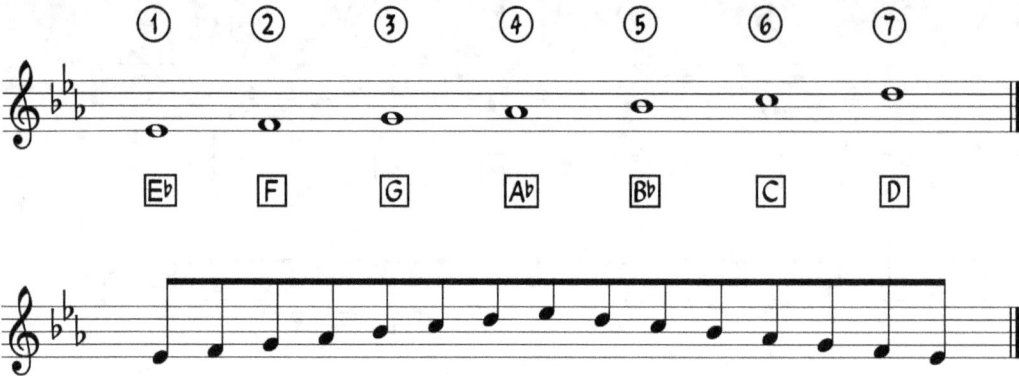

Key of E

Key of F

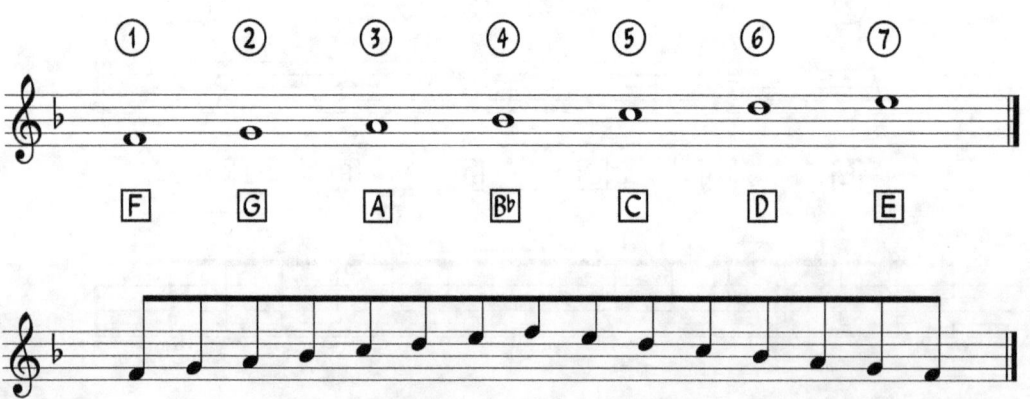

Key of F#

Key of G

Key of A♭

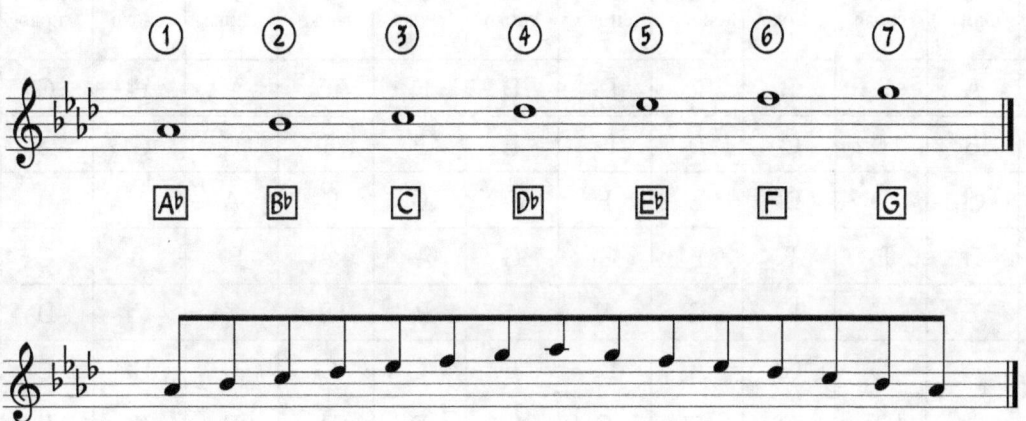

Using Numerals

At times, you will hear musicians make references to chords as being the four chord or the five chord, and you'll see this written as 'IV', 'II' or 'V' etc. So why is this? Roman numerals are a simple way of expressing which chord to use and have the advantage of not being set in any one key. Each number refers to a degree of a major scale which then tells you which chord is required. Each chord ('I' or 'V') will then vary depending on which key the music is in.

Example In Key Of 'C'

The chart below shows the numerals and their corresponding degrees of a scale, along with the relevant chords they refer to. This example being in the key of 'C'.

NUMERAL	DEGREE	CHORD IN 'C'
I	FIRST	C
II	SECOND	D
III	THIRD	E
IV	FOURTH	F
V	FIFTH	G
VI	SIXTH	A
VII	SEVENTH	B

Chart showing numerals with corresponding chord to each key.

NUMERAL	A CHORD	B♭ CHORD	B CHORD	C CHORD	D♭ CHORD	D CHORD	E♭ CHORD	E CHORD	F CHORD	F# CHORD	G CHORD	A♭ CHORD
I	A	B♭	B	C	D♭	D	E♭	E	F	F#	G	A♭
II	B	C	C#	D	E♭	E	F	F#	G	G#	A	B♭
III	C#	D	D#	E	F	F#	G	G#	A	A#	B	C
IV	D	E♭	E	F	G♭	G	A♭	A	B♭	B	C	D♭
V	E	F	F#	G	A♭	A	B♭	B	C	C#	D	E♭
VI	F#	G	G#	A	B♭	B	C	C#	D	D#	E	F
VII	G#	A	A#	B	C	C#	D	D#	E	E#	F	F#

The chords predominantly used in traditional blues music are the 'I' 'IV' and 'V' chords. It is important to commit these three chords to memory, ideally their use will become entirely automatic, without any thought, as this then allows for better improvisation. The chart shows each of the three chords for all keys, use this as reference but commit them to memory over a period time.

KEY	I CHORD	IV CHORD	V CHORD
A	A	D	E
B♭	B♭	E♭	F
B	B	E	G♭
C	C	F	G
D♭	D♭	G♭	A♭
D	D	G	A
E♭	E♭	A♭	B♭
E	E	A	B
F	F	B♭	C
F♯	F♯	B	C♯
G	G	C	D
A♭	A♭	D♭	E♭

12-Bar Chord Progressions

The most common chord progression for blues music is the twelve bar progression, hence the term 12-bar blues. This isn't the only chord structure used, but it is the most common.

12-Bar Progression

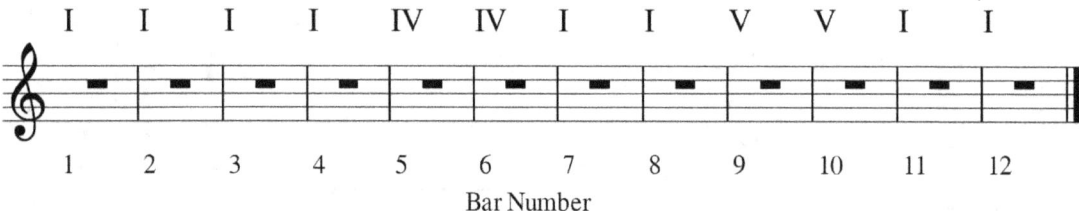

This is a standard twelve bar chord progression. It uses the 'I' 'IV' and 'V' chords. You can see the advantage of having been written with Roman numerals, as this is now open to being used in any key you choose.

Progression Breakdown

- 4 Bars of the 'I' chord   Bars 1 - 4
- 2 Bars of the 'IV' chord   Bars 5 - 6
- 2 Bars of the 'I' chord   Bars 7 - 8
- 2 Bars of the 'V' chord   Bars 9 - 10
- 2 Bars of the 'I' chord   Bars 11 - 12

That's the basic structure of a 12-bar blues, so now lets put this into some sort of context with some chords.

12-bar blues in 'C'

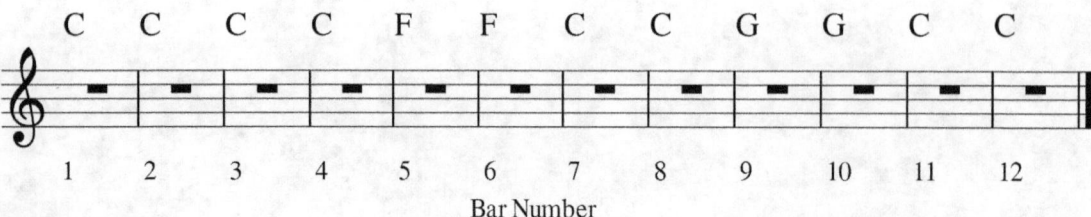

12-bar blues in 'A'

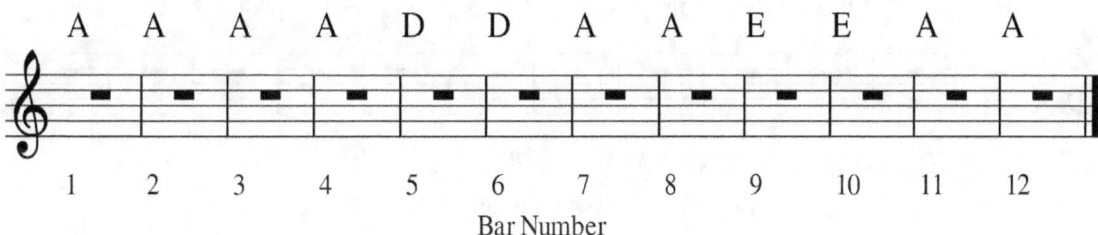

12-bar blues in 'B♭'

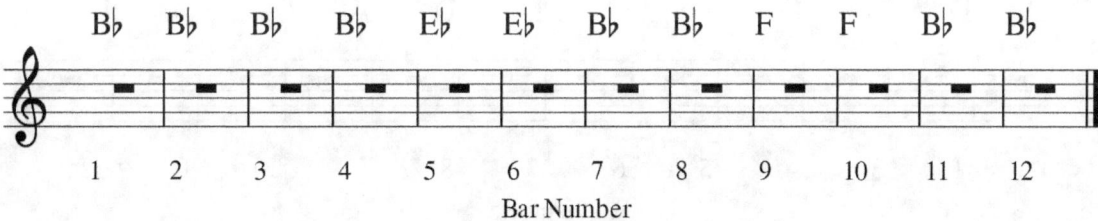

12-bar blues in 'B'

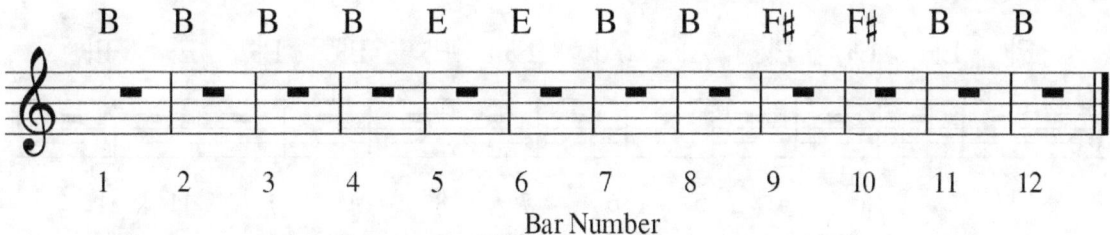

12-bar blues in 'C'

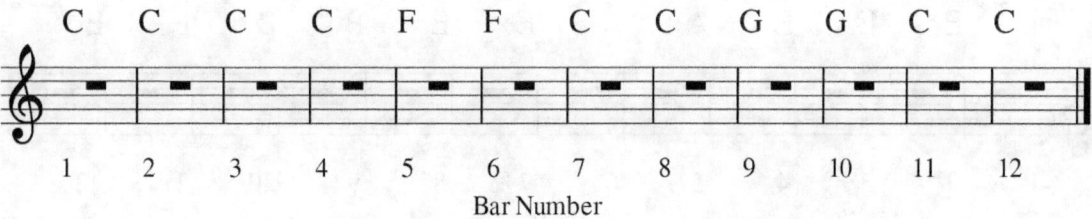

12-bar blues in 'D♭'

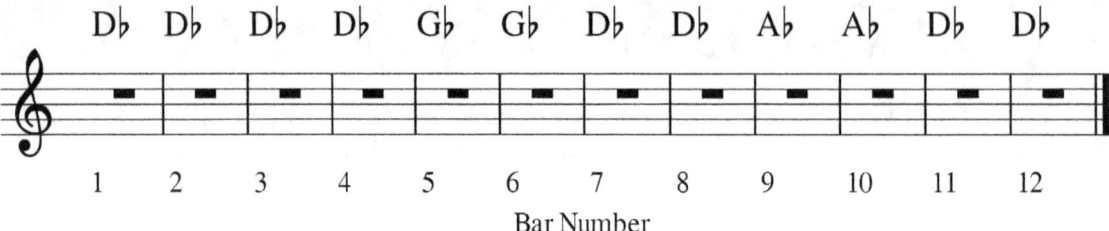

12-bar blues in 'D'

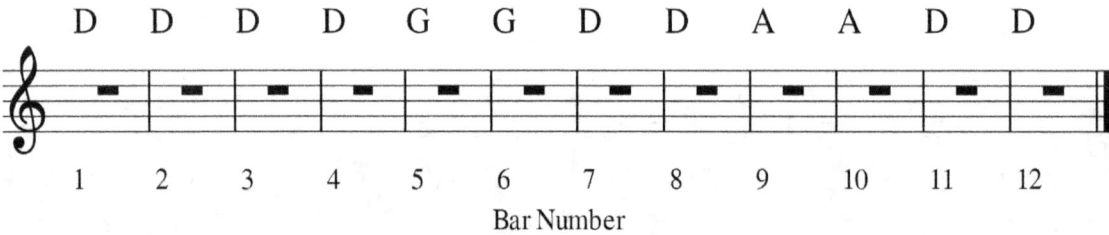

12-bar blues in 'E♭'

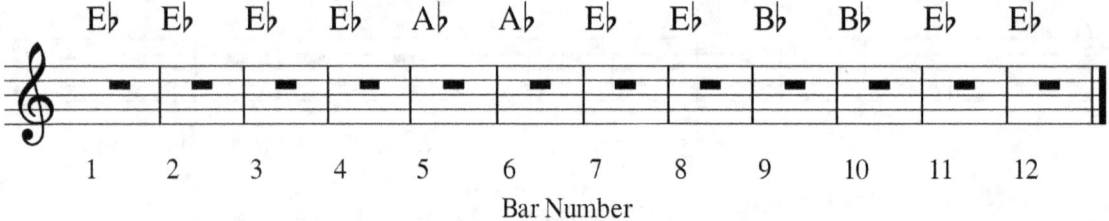

12-bar blues in 'E'

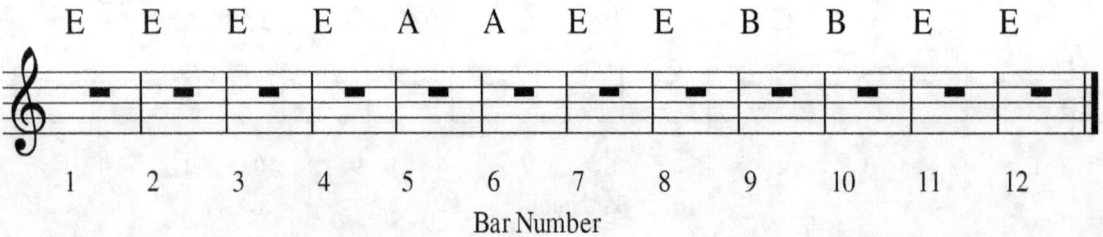

12-bar blues in 'F'

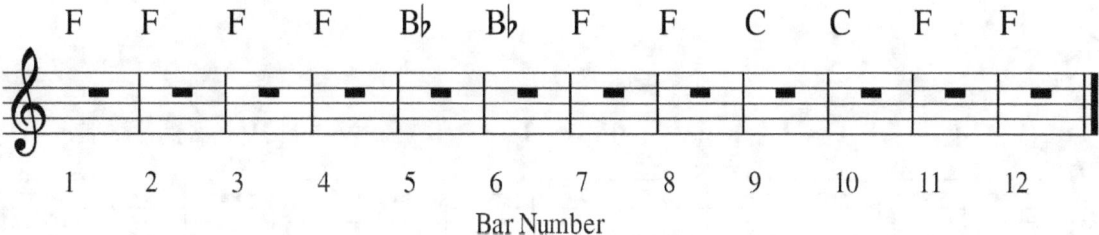

12-bar blues in 'F#'

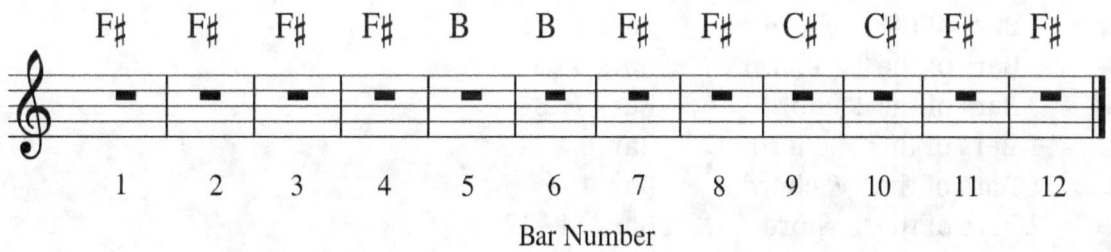

12-bar blues in 'G'

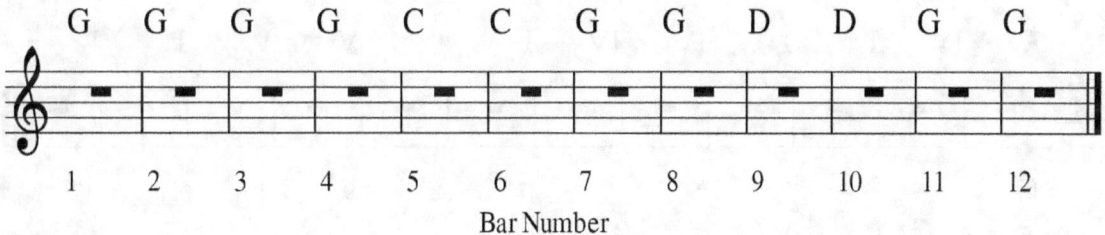

12-bar blues in 'A♭'

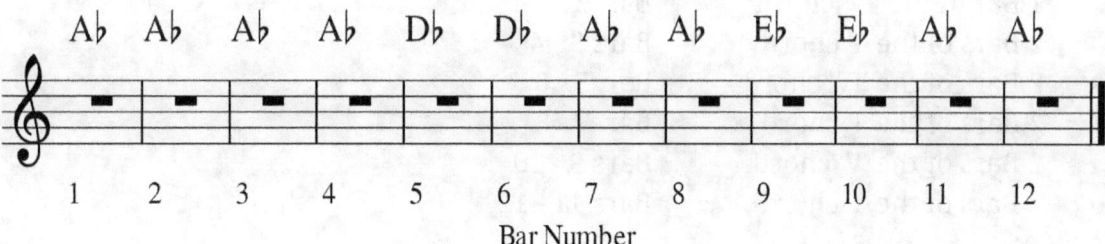

There are a number of variations of the 12-bar chord progression, here are some of the more commonly used ones. Shown as Roman numerals rather than chords.

1.

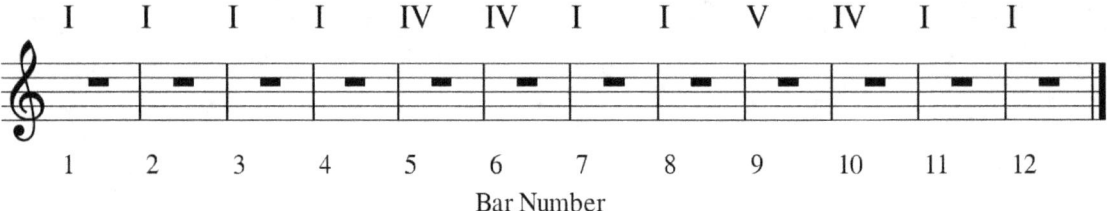

Progression Breakdown

- 4 Bars of the 'I' chord   Bars 1 - 4
- 2 Bars of the 'IV' chord   Bars 5 - 6
- 2 Bars of the 'I' chord   Bars 7 - 8
- 1 Bars of the 'V' chord   Bar 9
- 1 Bars of the 'IV' chord   Bar 10
- 2 Bars of the 'I' chord   Bars 11 - 12

2.

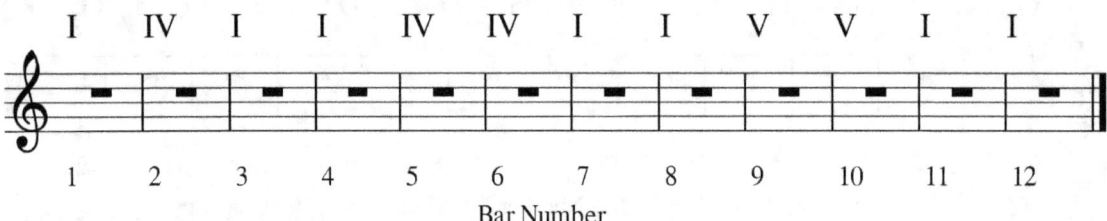

Progression Breakdown

- 1 Bar of the 'I' chord   Bar 1
- 1 Bar of the 'IV' chord   Bar 2
- 2 Bars of the 'I' chord   Bars 3 - 4
- 2 Bars of the 'IV' chord   Bar 5 - 6
- 2 Bars of the 'I' chord   Bar 7 - 8
- 2 Bars of the 'V' chord   Bars 9 - 10
- 2 Bars of the 'I' chord   Bars 11 - 12

3.

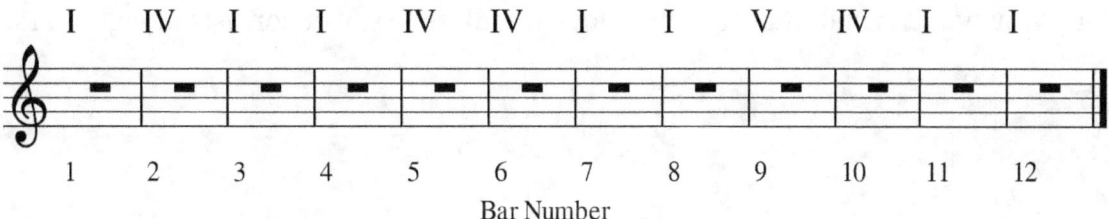

Progression Breakdown

- 1 Bar of the 'I' chord   Bar 1
- 1 Bar of the 'IV' chord   Bar 2
- 2 Bars of the 'I' chord   Bars 3 - 4
- 2 Bars of the 'IV' chord   Bar 5 - 6
- 2 Bars of the 'I' chord   Bar 7 - 8
- 1 Bar of the 'V' chord   Bar 9
- 1 Bar of the 'IV' chord   Bar 10
- 2 Bars of the 'I' chord   Bars 11 - 12

4.

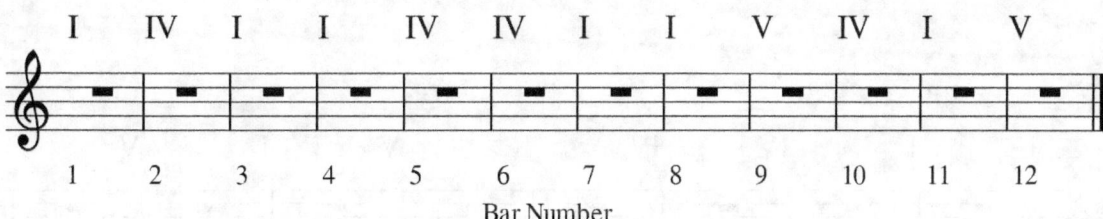

Progression Breakdown

- 1 Bar of the 'I' chord   Bar 1
- 1 Bar of the 'IV' chord   Bar 2
- 2 Bars of the 'I' chord   Bars 3 - 4
- 2 Bars of the 'IV' chord   Bar 5 - 6
- 2 Bars of the 'I' chord   Bar 7 - 8
- 1 Bar of the 'V' chord   Bar 9
- 1 Bar of the 'IV' chord   Bar 10
- 1 Bar of the 'I' chord   Bars 11
- 1 Bar of the 'V' chord   Bar 12

8-Bar Chord Progressions

The 8-bar blues is another traditional form, although it isn't quite as prevalent as the 12-bar format, it is still important to know. Needless to say, it consists of eight bars.

1.

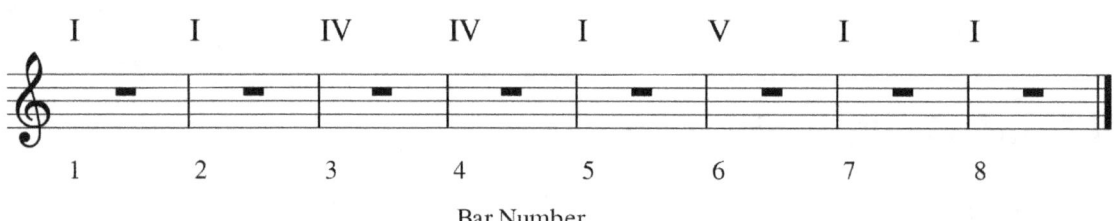

Progression Breakdown

- 2 Bars of the 'I' chord   Bar 1 - 2
- 2 Bars of the 'IV' chord   Bar 3 - 4
- 1 Bar of the 'I' chord   Bar 5
- 1 Bars of the 'V' chord   Bar 6
- 2 Bars of the 'I' chord   Bar 7 - 8

2.

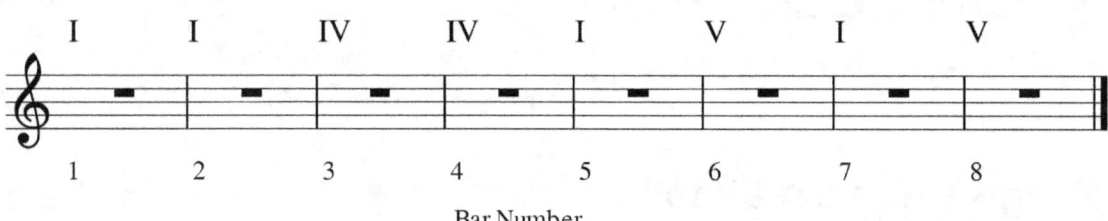

Progression Breakdown

- 2 Bars of the 'I' chord   Bar 1 - 2
- 2 Bars of the 'IV' chord   Bar 3 - 4
- 1 Bar of the 'I' chord   Bar 5
- 1 Bars of the 'V' chord   Bar 6
- 1 Bar of the 'I' chord   Bar 7
- 1 Bar of the 'V' chord   Bar 8

3.

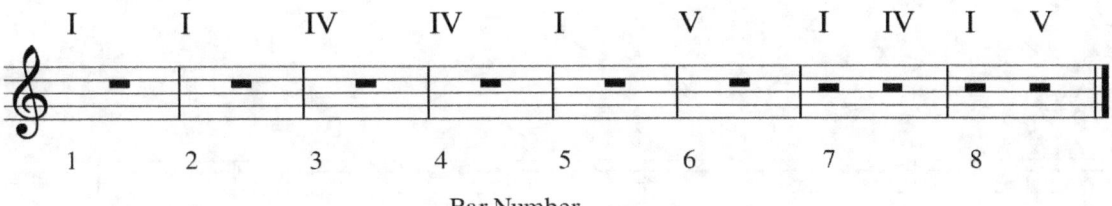

Progression Breakdown

- 2 Bars of the 'I' chord   Bar 1 - 2
- 2 Bars of the 'IV' chord   Bar 3 - 4
- 1 Bar of the 'I' chord   Bar 5
- 1 Bars of the 'V' chord   Bar 6
- ½ Bar of the 'I' chord   Bar 7
- ½ Bar of the 'IV' chord   Bar 7
- ½ Bar of the 'I' chord   Bar 8
- ½ Bar of the 'V' chord   Bar 8

4.

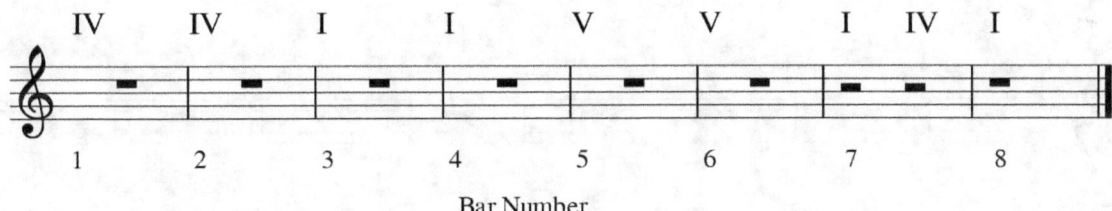

Progression Breakdown

- 2 Bars of the 'IV' chord   Bar 1 - 2
- 2 Bars of the 'I' chord   Bar 3 - 4
- 2 Bars of the 'V' chord   Bar 5 - 6
- ½ Bar of the 'I' chord   Bar 7
- ½ Bar of the 'IV' chord   Bar 7
- 1 Bar of the 'I' chord   Bar 8

16-Bar Chord Progressions

The 16-bar blues has various forms, these two could be seen as adaptions from the 12-bar format with extra 'I' chord sections in place.

1.

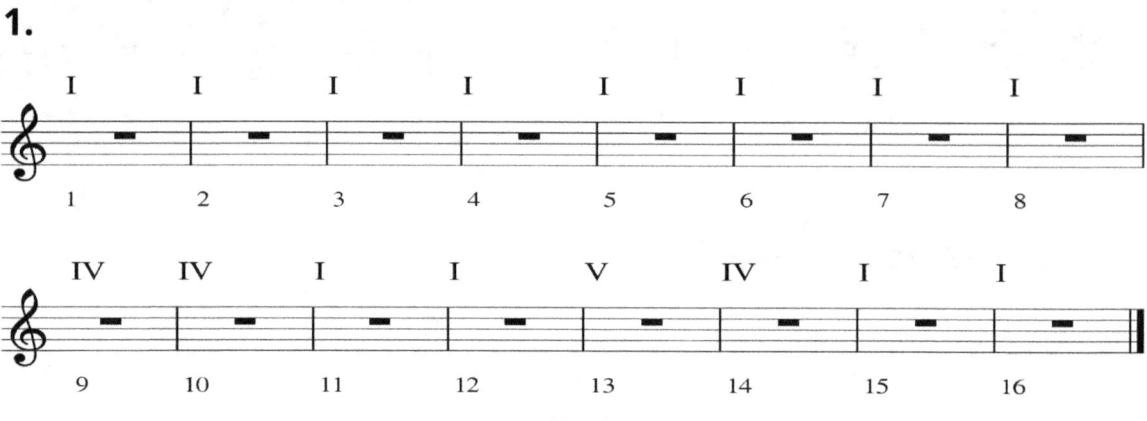

Progression Breakdown

- 4 Bars of the 'I' chord   Bar 1 - 8
- 2 Bars of the 'IV' chord   Bar 9 - 10
- 2 Bars of the 'I' chord   Bar 11 - 12
- 1 Bar of the 'V' chord   Bar 13
- 1 Bar of the 'IV' chord   Bar 14
- 2 Bars of the 'I' chord   Bar 15 - 16

2.

Progression Breakdown

- 8 Bars of the 'I' chord   Bar 1 - 8
- 2 Bars of the 'IV' chord   Bar 9 - 10
- 2 Bars of the 'I' chord   Bar 11 – 12
- 1 Bar of the 'V' chord   Bar 13
- 1 Bar of the 'IV' chord   Bar 14
- 2 Bars of the 'I' chord   Bar 15 - 16

Fingering/Audio

Some examples within the book will offer fingering suggestions. These all follow the standard numbering system. Both thumbs are always referred to as being number one, with both the little fingers being number five. Naturally, no two peoples hands are exactly the same, so any suggestions must always be taken as such, suggestions. With different hand sizes, spans, widths, spacing between fingers and the hands' ability to stretch varying so much, what is comfortable for one person, won't necessary work for another.

Finger Numbering

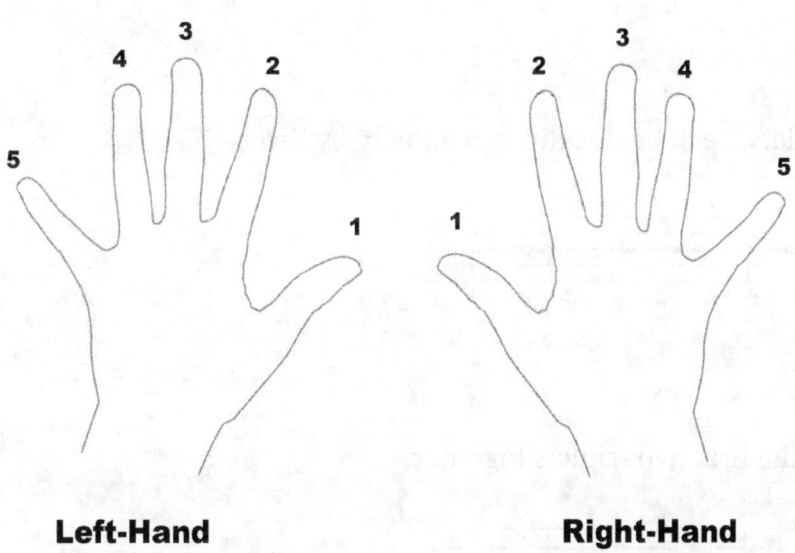

Left-Hand   Right-Hand

Audio Examples

The examples that have audio to accompany them, can be identified by having the relevant number next to an audio sign. For access, refer to page 233, for information regarding downloading them from the website.

Example Accompanying Audio Sign

Blues Shuffle Feel

Blues is generally played with a shuffle/swing feel, which is to say it uses a lot of triplet timing. This is more often than not notated as 4/4 although sometimes 12/8. But what is a shuffle feel?

Straight 4/4 timing, with four beats per bar.

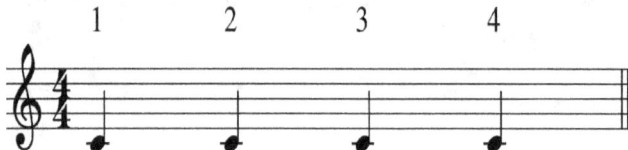

4/4 timing using triplets. Each beat is divided equally by three.

The shuffle feel ties the first two triplets together.

If you are new to triplet timing, just remember that each beat is divided by three, so count 1-2-3 over each individual beat.

The same applies with the shuffle feel, even though the first note is held longer.

The shuffle feel used in blues music can be seen to be notated in several ways, some technically correct, while others simply imply the shuffle/swing feel.

1.

This is technically correct, with the use of actual triplets.

2.

The use of dotted quavers and semi-quavers is often used, this gives the notation the impression of the shuffle feel, although if played as written, it would sound very strange and awkward and unnatural.

3.

Being notated with completely straight quavers is obviously not correct, but you will see this along with a sign that informs you that the quavers actually denote something else.

> Given time and practice, all of these will mean much the same to you, and the shuffle feel will become a natural thing without any thought being involved, regardless of how it has been notated.

Chords/Triads

A triad is a three note chord, the simplest being the major chord, along with the minor, augmented and diminished chords. The major chord is really the building block of all other chords, in a sense they just have notes added or altered.

Shown is the 'C' major scale. A basic major chord is created from the 1st (root note) 3rd and 5th degrees of a major scale.

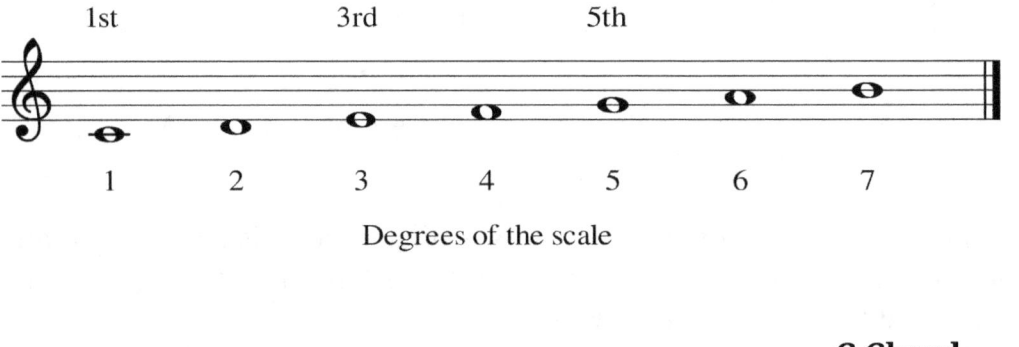

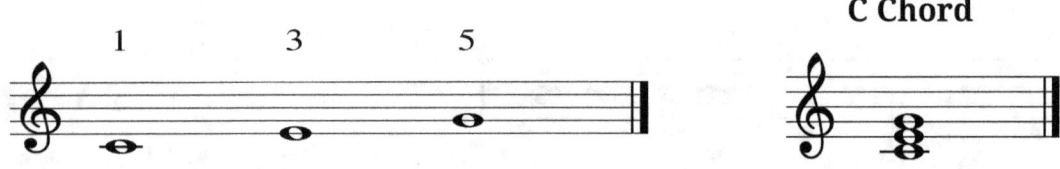

Taking the 1st - 3rd - 5th degrees of this major scale creates the 'C' major chord. Having three notes, there are three possible ways of playing this, or three inversion.

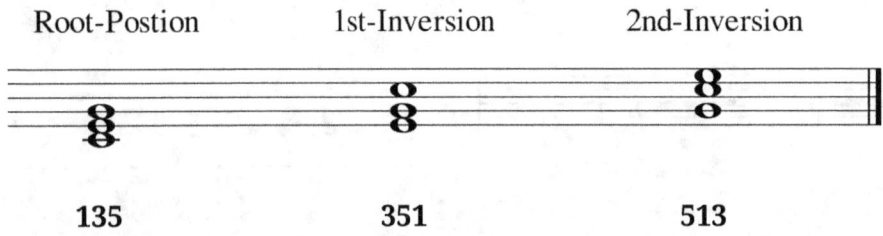

The numbers below the chords refer to the scale degrees, written in order as played. Always remember to use different inversions of chords in your improvisation and not stick to the same comfortable ones that you tend to automatically go to.

Chords 6ths

A six chord is a major chord with the addition of the 6th degree of the major scale.

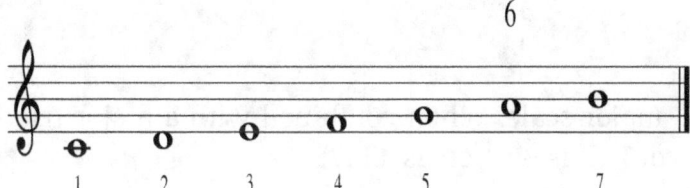

The 6th degree of a major scale is the sixth note along when counting from the root note.

So in order to form a six chord, take a major chord and add the 6th. In this case we are looking at the 'C' scale and the chord 'C6'.

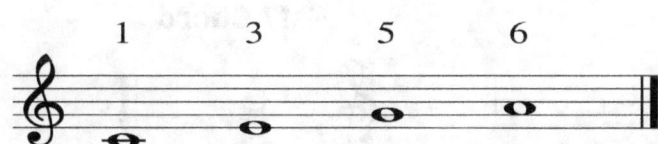

C6 Chord

Because a six chord is a four note chord, there are therefore four different possible positions/inversions that it can be played in. The numbers below the chords refer to the scale degrees written in order as played.

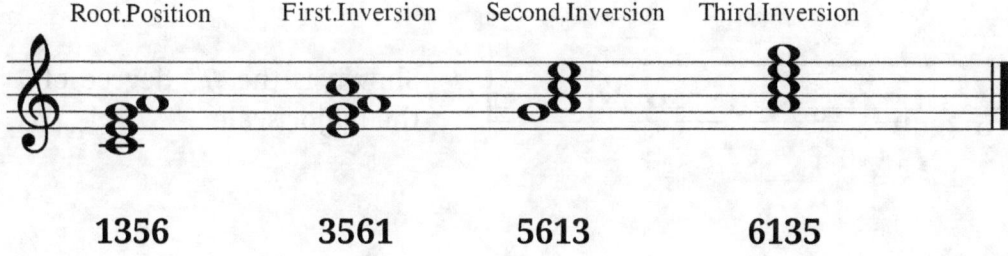

Chord 7ths

The next chord to look at is the seven, or more specifically the dominant seventh chord, as it is this and not the major seventh that is generally used within the blues.

Major Seventh Chord

Below shows the 7th degree of a 'C' major scale. When combined with a major triad this creates the 'C' major seven chord. This is written as 'CM7'.

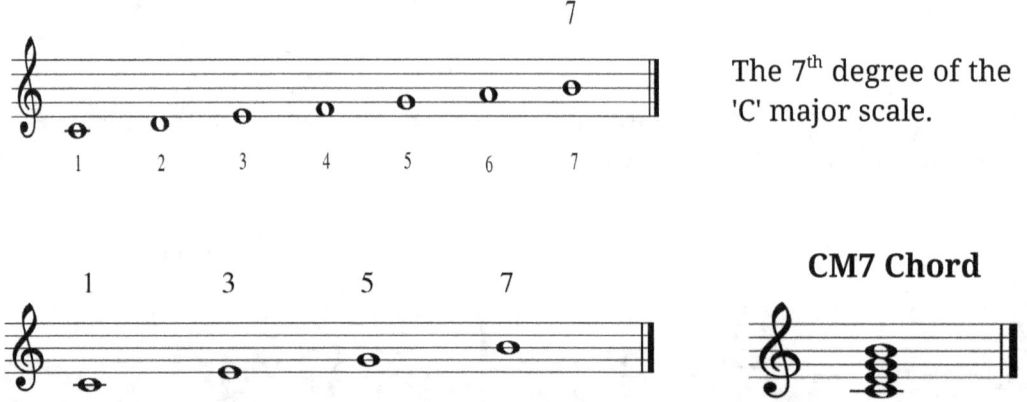

The 7th degree of the 'C' major scale.

CM7 Chord

Dominant Seventh Chord

As the major seventh isn't generally used, when you hear a seven being mentioned it will instead refer to the dominant seventh shown below. This is simply the major seventh but flattened. This is written as 'C7'.

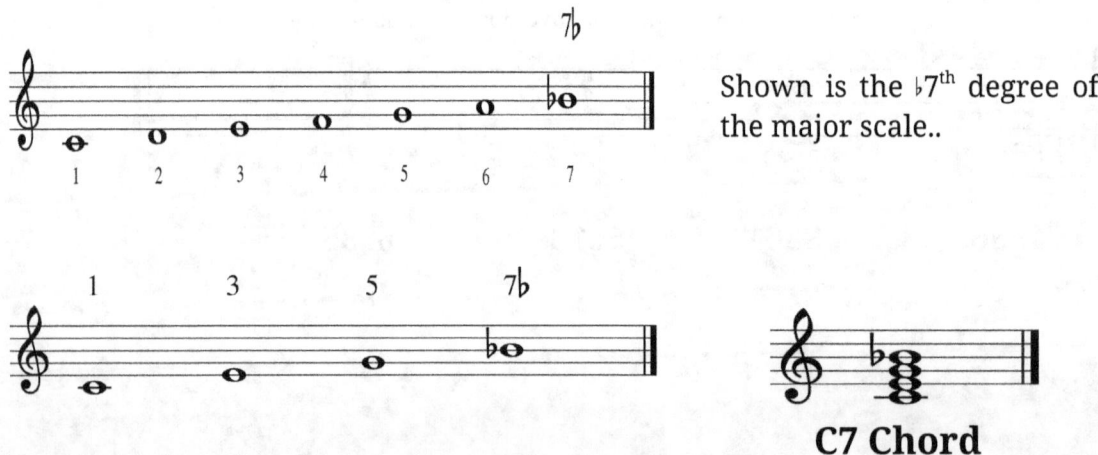

Shown is the ♭7th degree of the major scale..

C7 Chord

The dominant seven chords are created from four notes, therefore it has four possible inversions (positions it can be played). Shown below are all four inversions for the I - IV - V chords in the key of 'C'.

C7

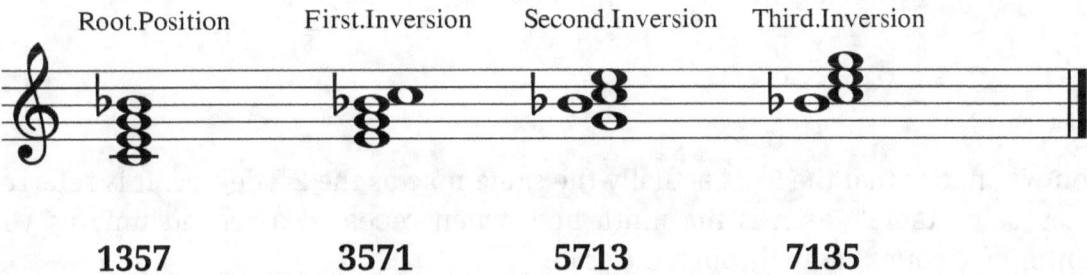

| 1357 | 3571 | 5713 | 7135 |

F7

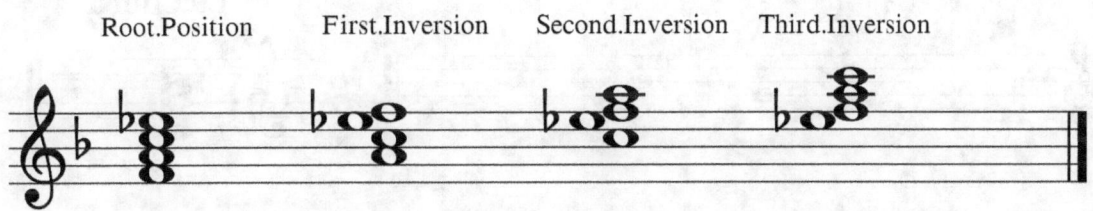

G7

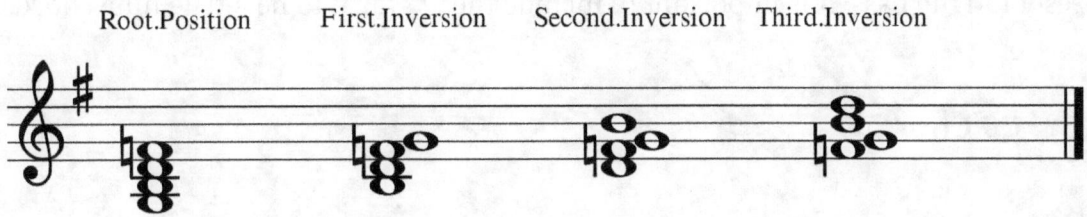

> It is important to get used to using every inversion of every chord, as this allows for easier improvisation and more variation in your playing. The numbers below the chords refer to the scale degrees, written in order as played.

Chord 9ths

Next is the nine chord. The nine is slightly more involved in that it builds upon the seven chord. Below shows the 9th degree within a 'C' major scale.

You will notice that the 9th is actually the same note as the 2nd degree. It is referred to as being the 9th, as it is the ninth note when repeated a second time as you continue to count on up through the scale.

Below shows the 'C9' chord. This is essentially a 'C7' with an added 9th note.

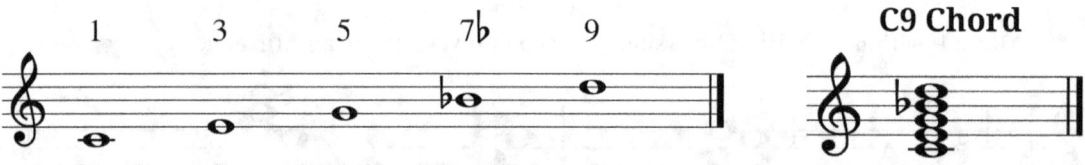

You will notice that this chord consists of five notes instead of four, which would makes its use quite difficult. Therefore, it is usual to omit a note, creating a four note chord once again. This is most commonly the root note, as the root is already present in the bass. It is important to include the b7th for it to be a true nine chord.

3579

The C9 chord as it is more likely to be played, with the root note having been removed.

The nine chord is now created from four notes (with the root being omitted) therefore it has four possible inversions (positions it can be played). Shown below are all four inversions for the I - IV - V chords. Note that although it says root position, the root note is omitted.

C9

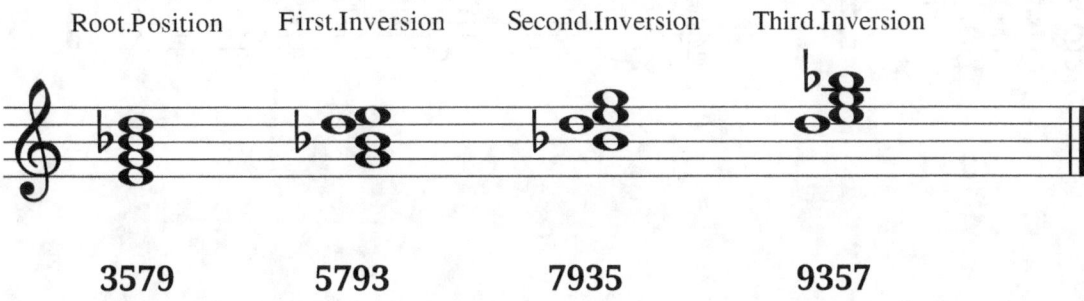

| 3579 | 5793 | 7935 | 9357 |

F9

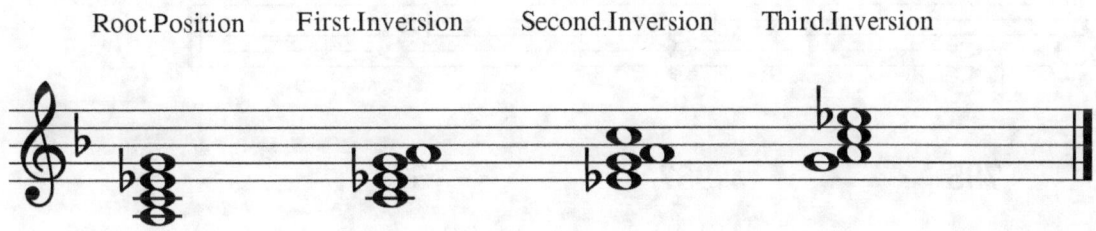

G9

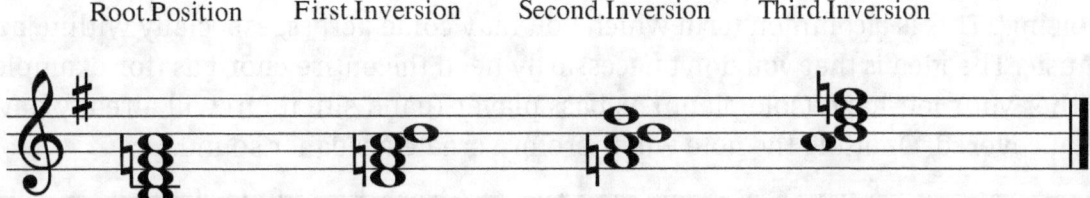

> Although the (rootless) root position chord is probably the most common, it's important to be familiar with all versions of a chord, as this allows for more varied improvisation when playing. The numbers below the chords refer to the scale degrees, written in order as played.

There are other ways to play the nine chord. With the option of using a three note or even a two note voicing. A common three note voicing omits the 1st/root and the 3rd to create the chord below.

795

Three Possible Positions/Inversions

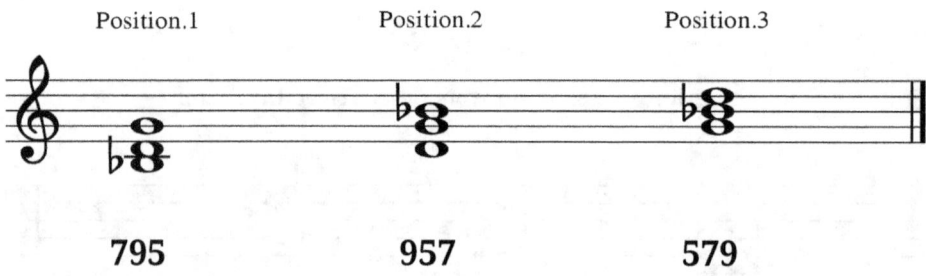

795   **957**   **579**

> A chord that does not include the root note is often referred to as being a 'rootless voicing'. This is a common term which you may come across, especially within jazz music. The idea is that you don't necessarily need the entire chord as (for example) either your left-hand (solo piano) or bass player (band situation) will already have that covered. Omitting the note will therefore create a cleaner sound.

With a rootless chord voicing you can omit the notes in the right-hand that the left-hand is already playing, as the two together will complete the chord. The ninth (being a larger chord) is more likely to be used in this way. Bear in mind that it helps to keep the identity of the chord if the bass contains the root note.

Take a rootless 'C9' chord. Without the root (on either the right-hand or the left) its identity is unclear. A quick look will confirm that it could be mistaken for 'Gm6'.

A rootless 'C9' shown to be the same as the 'Gm6' chord. Being 1-3♭-5-6 of the 'G' major scale. You can see without the root, it can be mistaken for a different chord.

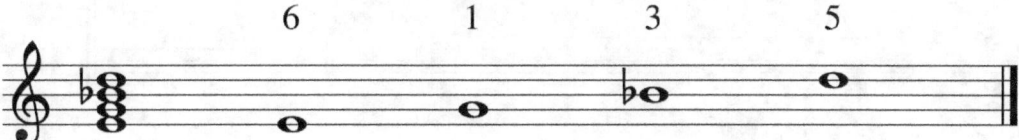

But with the simple inclusion of the root note in the bass, its identity is confirmed as being 'C9'. So the root note here in the right-hand is not really necessary. The combination of both left and right hands completing a chord could be referred to as being a two-handed voicing.

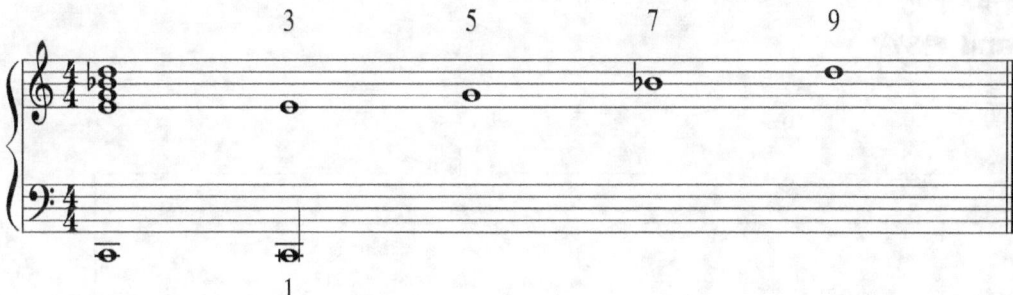

Further examples of a two-handed voicing would need to consist of a fuller left-hand and a lighter right-hand. Below shows the chord with a 3-2 split, 3 notes in the right-hand and 2 notes in the left-hand.

Right-hand 379
Left-hand   15

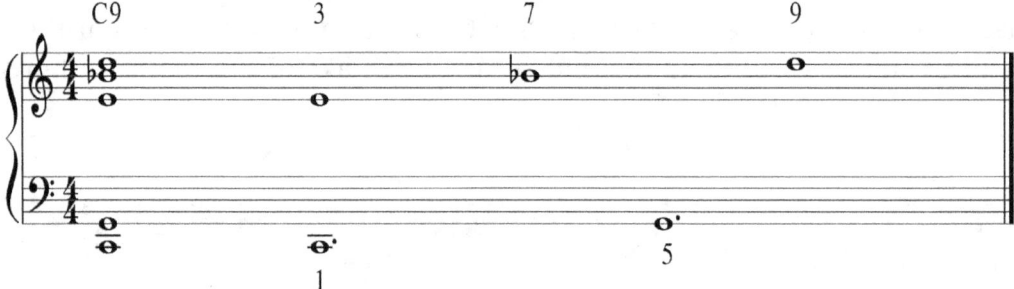

Or another example, swap things around with a 2-3 split, 2 notes in the right-hand and 3 notes in the left-hand.

Right-hand 95
Left-hand   137

Chord 13ths

The next chord is the thirteen. If you count up the major scale to the 13th degree you will find that this is the same note as the 6th. The thirteen chord is essentially a major chord with both the 6th and the 7th. You will notice that these two numbers also happen to add up to thirteen.

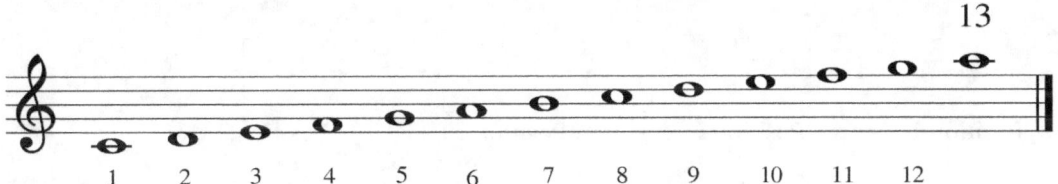

When you form the chord it is easier to think of it as being a seven chord with an added sixth. Shown below is the chord in its entirety, although you won't actually play it as such as it contains five notes.

Much like the nine chords, the thirteen is normally played with a note omitted, again this is normally the root. Perhaps obviously both the 6th and the 7th (much like with the nine chords) should be present.

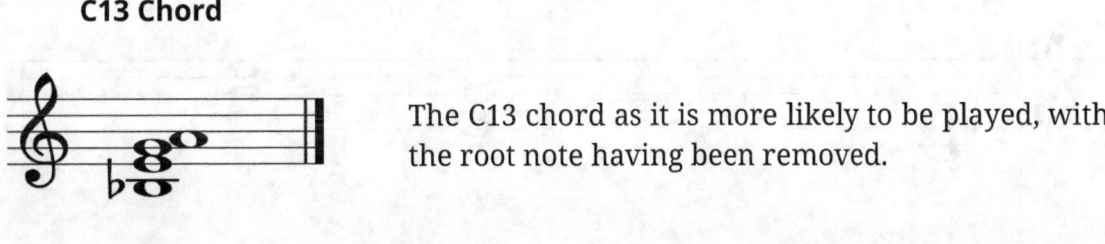

The C13 chord as it is more likely to be played, with the root note having been removed.

The thirteen chord is now created from four notes (with the root being omitted) therefore it has four possible inversions (positions which it can be played). Shown below are all four inversions for the I - IV - V chords in the key of 'C'. The numbers below the chords refer to the scale degrees, written in order as played.

C13

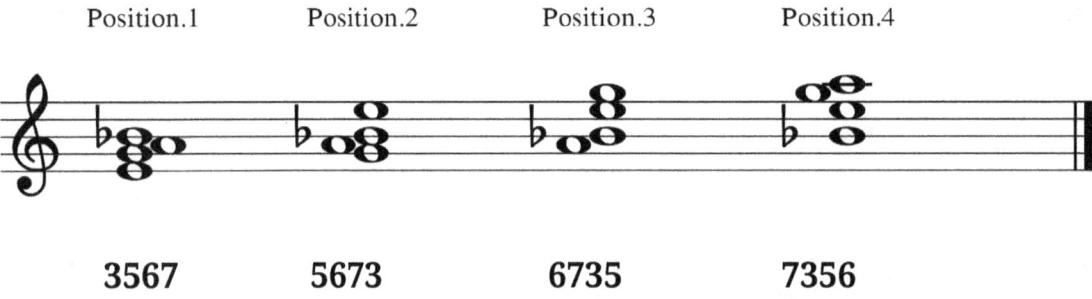

    3567   **5673**   **6735**   **7356**

F13

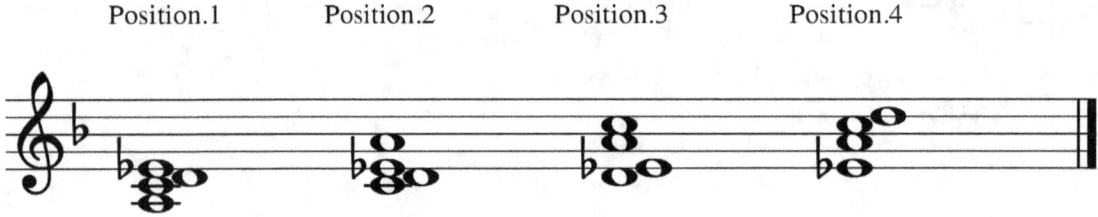

G13

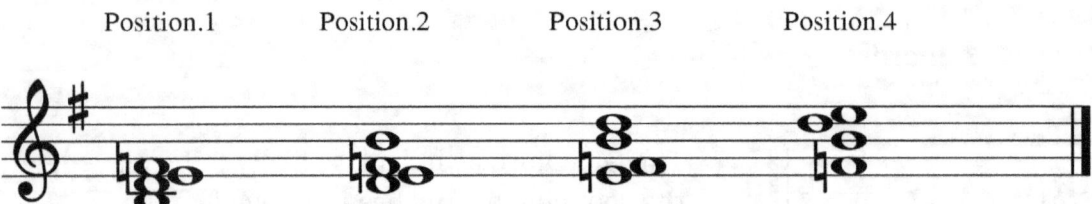

The thirteen chord is often played with the 9th as an addition. This normally requires another note to be omitted to keep it down to only four notes, this is usually the 5th. This is a great, full sounding chord that begs to be resolved down.

Below shows C13 add 9 in four different possible positions/inversions.

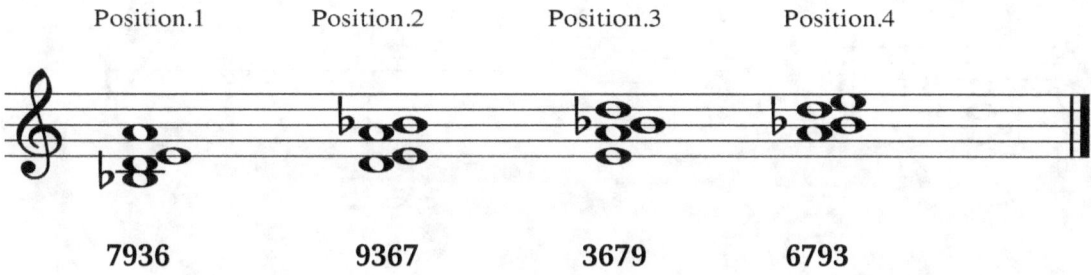

With a two-handed voicing of this, the left-hand can fill in the missing harmonics, being the 1st/root and 5th, so giving you the complete chord.

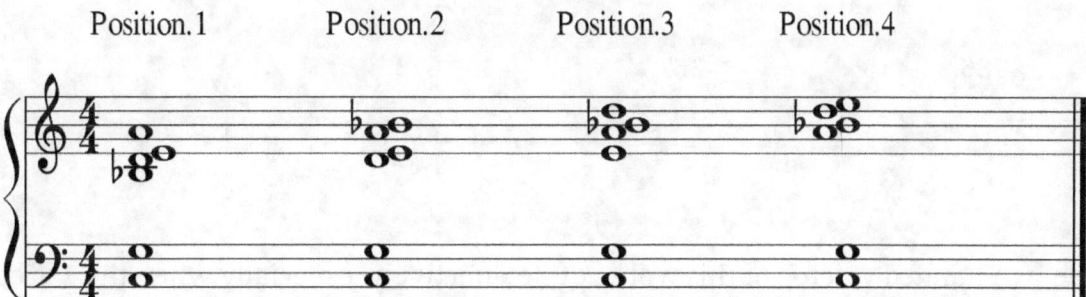

Although the thirteenth chord is five notes in its complete form you can simplify it down to three notes at times, creating a sharper, cleaner sound.

The thirteenth chord with the root and fifth omitted. Leaving the 3rd, 6th and 7th. This works more effectively in some positions than others.

736

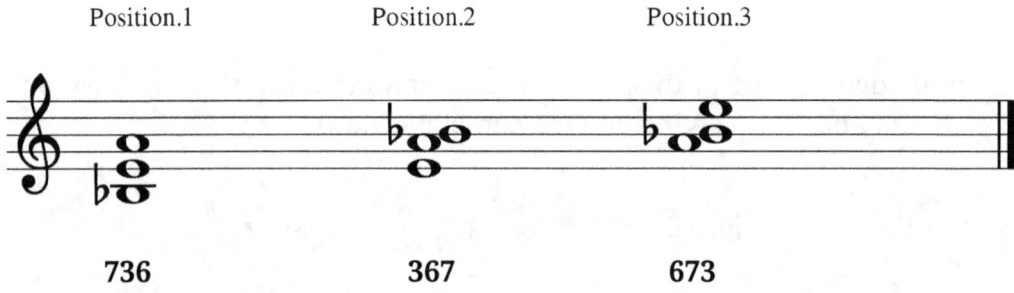

736   **367**   **673**

The two-handed voicing of this works quite effectively, especially when the 1st/root and 5th are commonly found in blues the left-hands.

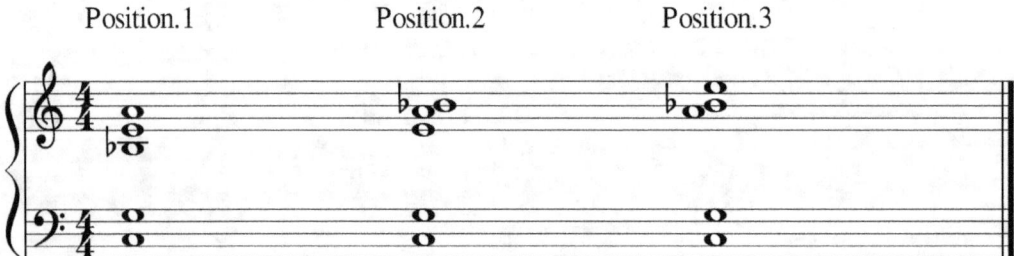

Rootless Chord Voicing

A rootless voicing is a chord that does not include the root note. This is a fundamental aspect of jazz piano and while this isn't a jazz book by any means, there is always a certain amount of cross-over and the use of rootless voicing can also work within the blues.

The purpose of rootless voicing is two-fold. For one, pianists often work with bass players who are already covering the root notes, therefore if the pianist over uses the root it could potentially lead to a slightly muddy sound. A rootless voicing by comparison provides quite a clean sound, which also better allows for the use of extensions to the said chord (An extension is an addition like a ninth or thirteenth). Secondly, in jazz certain chord progressions mean that with the rootless voicing there is very little movement required for the chord changes. This allows for a smoother more professional sounding performance. This isn't quite the case with twelve bar blues, but we can still make use of some nice sounding chords.

So how is a rootless voicing formed?

Step One

To begin with, select a chord to work with, in this case the chord 'C7'

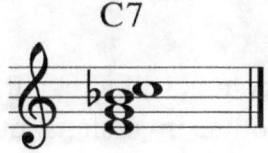

Different inversions of the 'C7' chord.

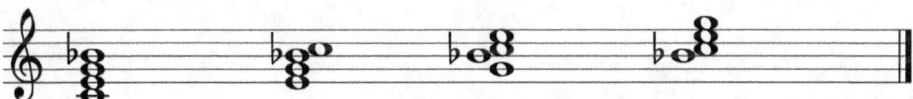

Step Two

Invert the chord so either the third or the seventh is the lowest note of the chord. This applies to major, minor or dominant chords.

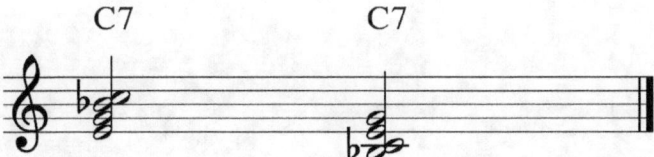

The first 'C7' chord has the third as the lowest note, the second chord has the seventh as the lowest note.

Step Three

Remove the root note from the chord.

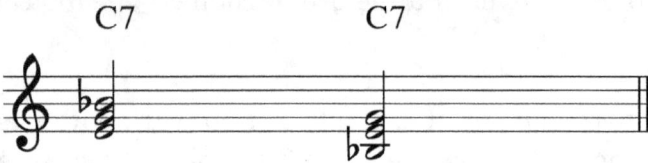

Step Four

Replace the missing root note with the 9th. So in essence the root is substituted with the 9th. And there you have it, a rootless voicing of the 'C7' chord.

Note that the 9th is placed in such a manner that the lowest note is still either the 3rd or the 7th. It is of course possible to play these chords in other inversions, but you lose a degree of clarity.

With dominant seventh chords (which is what we deal with a lot in the blues) you can also replace the 5th with the 13th.

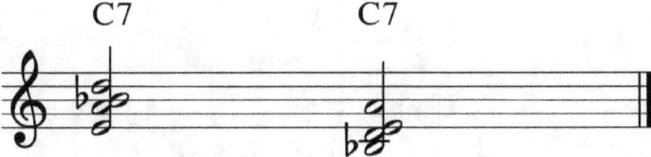

You can also play these as three note chords as well, by just omitting the 5th instead of substituting it for the 13th.

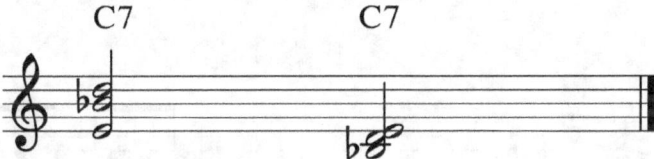

As you can see, the first chord with the 3rd as the lowest note works better, being nicely spaced out, compared to when the 7th is the lowest, creating a chord that is bunched up somewhat.

If you take a 7 - 3 interval (a 3rd and 7th played together) it is possible to build upon them to create a rootless voiced chord. When the 3rd is the lowest note you can add a 9th above it, shown below.

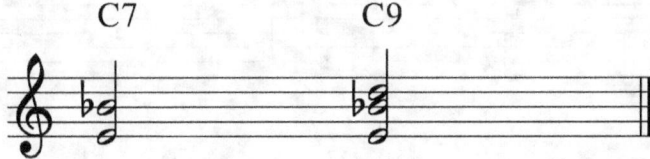

When the 7th is the lowest note, you can add a 13th above it, as shown below.

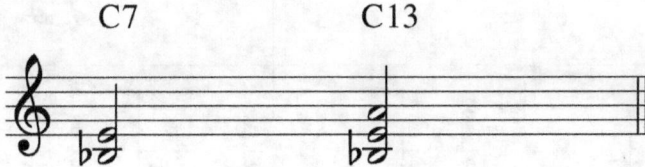

An example of a 12-bar blues, using mostly root-less voicing.

Scales For Blues

It could be said that knowing a few relevant scales is essential to playing the blues. Now on the one hand you don't want to get too obsessed and hung up on them as they can be misused, but then again they will help endlessly once absorbed, giving you an instant pool of improvisational possibilities.

When someone mentions scales regarding 'blues' music, most people will instantly think of the blues scale, but there isn't really one scale as such and even then it is an adaption of another scale. You may know or have heard of the 'pentatonic' scales, these are used a lot in popular western music and earn their name from the fact that they consist of five notes. There are both major and minor variations of this scale, both of which can be used in 'blues' music.

The scale that has earned its name as the 'blues scale' is actually not even considered to be a true scale at all, at least by traditional music theory. It is in-fact the minor pentatonic scale with a single added note, a so called 'blue' note. This extra note is considered to be an alternative inflection, and so not fitting the traditional definition of a scale. Although this is the more commonly known version, there is also a 'major blues scale' which is the 'major pentatonic' scale with a different 'blue note' or alternative inflection.

Learning these scales (real or otherwise) is essential to improvising as they are the building blocks of the blues, but be very careful with them. The problem being is it's very easy to learn them and then find yourself in a trap where you just run up and down them in parrot fashion, with the end results being a little dull and repetitive. Instead, when you learn them, learn to break them up into groups, using them as smaller sections. Also try switching from one to another or even combine them into one, making an endless stream of possibilities.

Nobody can learn every scale in every key instantly, it takes a lot of time. So start with the key or keys that you are currently working on, master them (to a degree) before you move on and try learning another key. Remember to practice them slowly until you know them intimately, don't try to play them fast, become comfortable with them first, get to know the notes, the patterns, and the feel over the keyboard as you play. Start with one octave up and down and then practice over two octaves and then three. I wouldn't spend ages practising them at anyone time, that might very well drive you insane, but practice them regularly, and eventually they will become second nature to you.

Major Pentatonic Scale

The major pentatonic scale is used in many forms of popular music, it is only five notes long, hence the term 'pentatonic'. The scale consists of the first, second, third, fifth, and sixth degrees of a major scale.

'C' Major Pentatonic Scale

Degrees 1 – 2 – 3 – 5 – 6

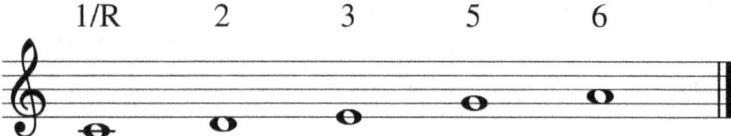

Another way of working out a scale rather than thinking in terms of degrees, is to think in terms of steps.

W – W – W+H – W

It is a good idea to practice over several octaves, start with one before practicing over two and then even three octaves, increasing it as you feel comfortable.

Major Pentatonic Scale (Key Of 'C') Over Two Octaves

Key of A

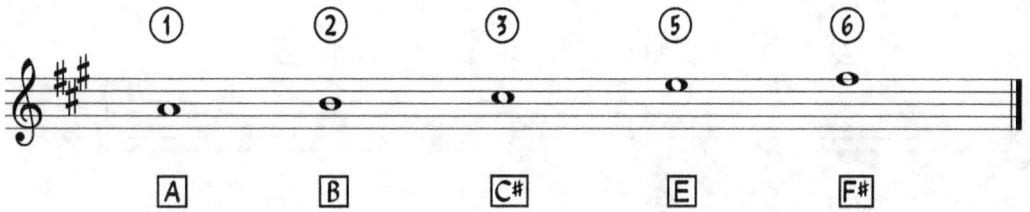

Key of B♭

Key of B

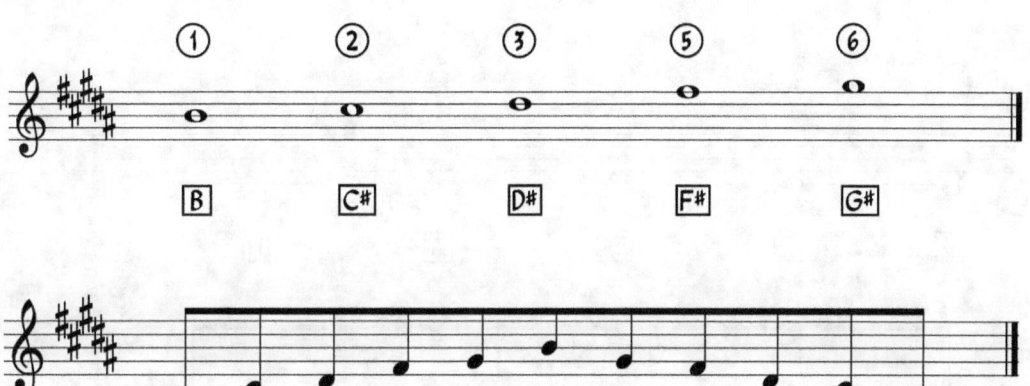

Key of C

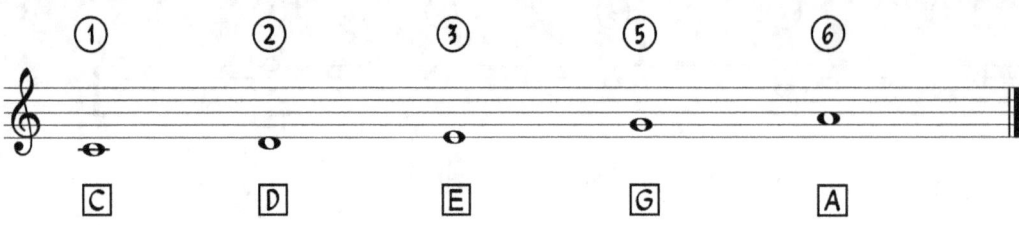

Key of D♭

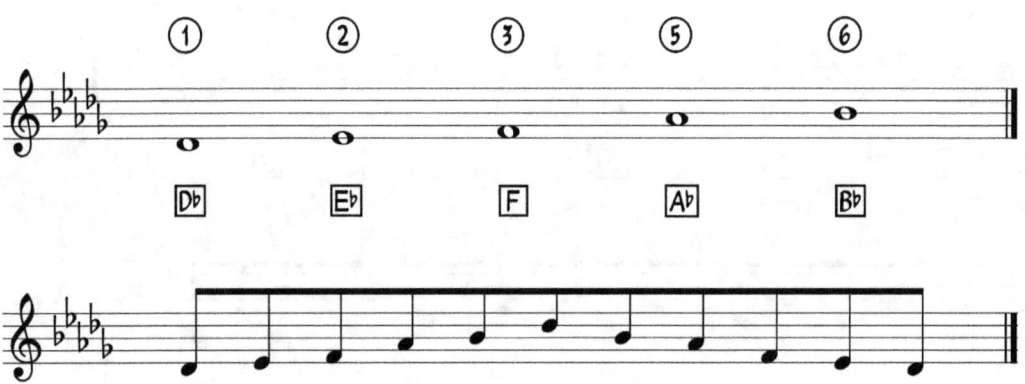

Key of D

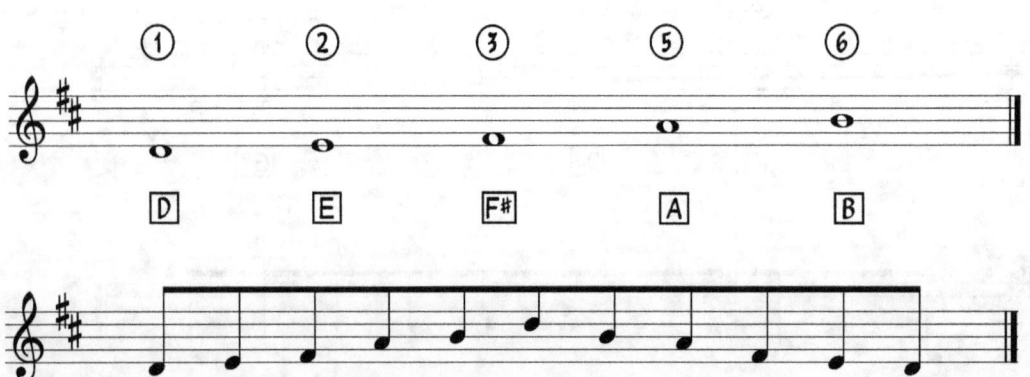

Key of E♭

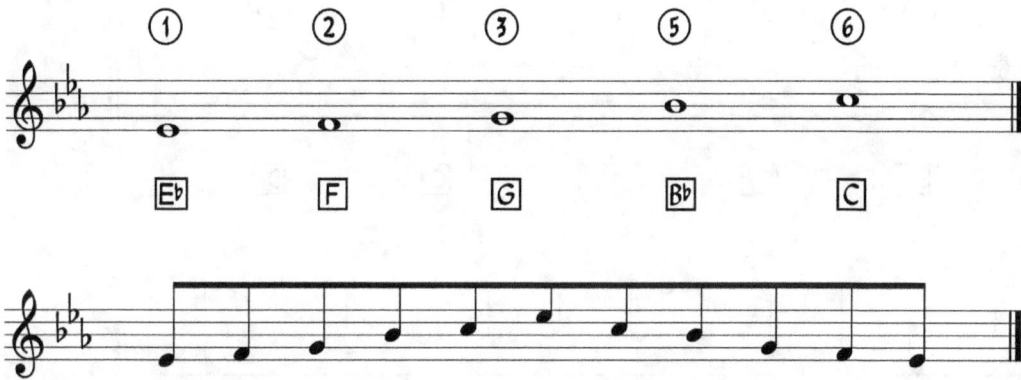

Key of E

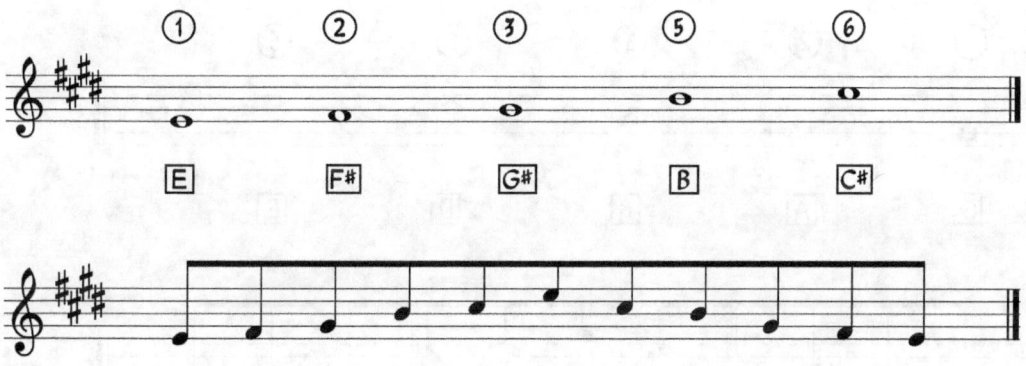

Key of F

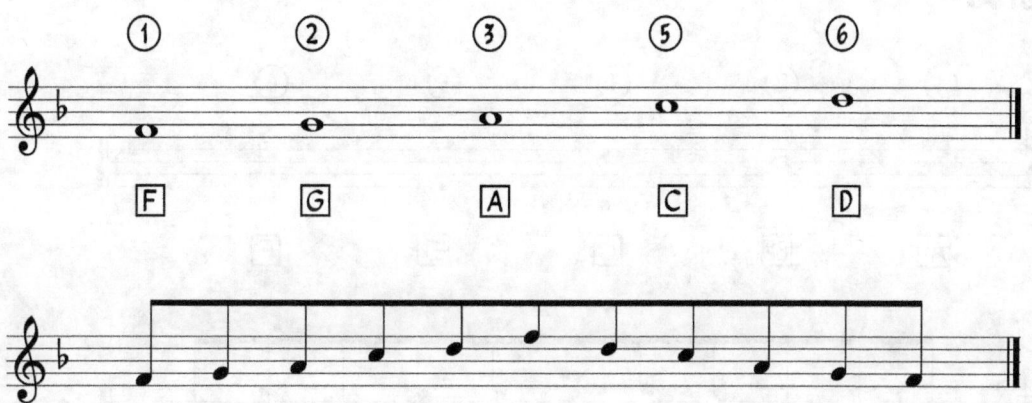

Key of F#

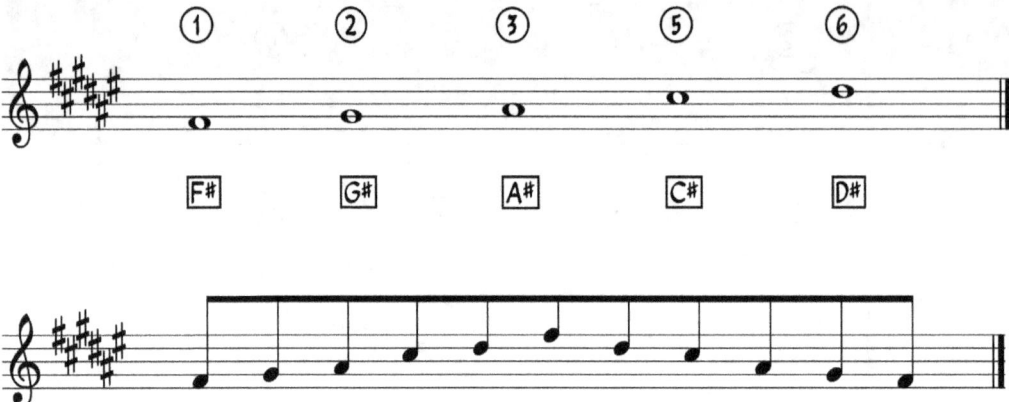

Key of G

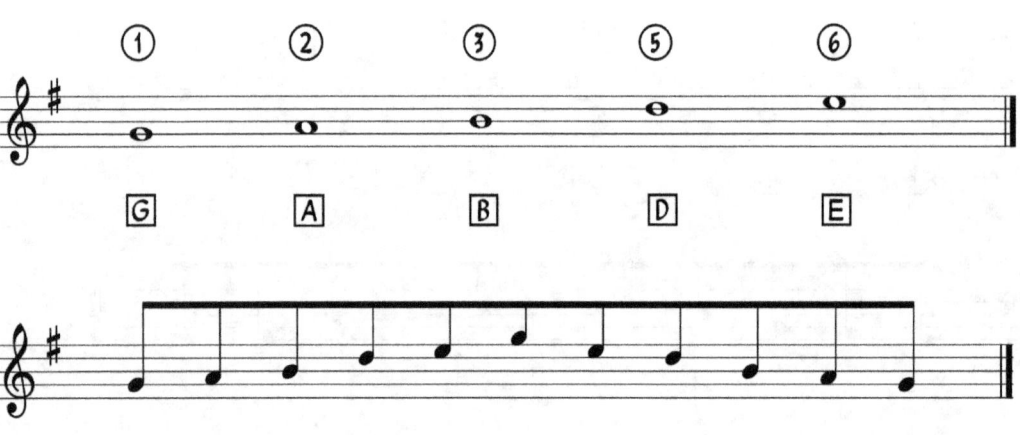

Key of A♭

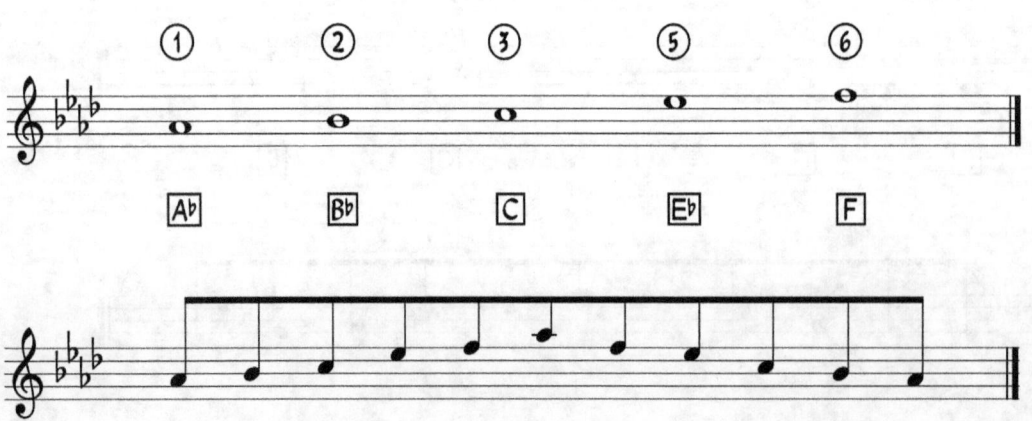

Major Blues Scale

The major blues scale is one of two scales that claim the title 'blues'. This is perhaps the slightly lesser known of the two, with the other being more commonly associated with blues. It is actually the major pentatonic scale with an additional note, that being the minor third. Traditional music theory doesn't really consider it a true scale at all, as it's the pentatonic with an added inflection, the so called 'blue note', but regardless of this, it doesn't change its use and existence in reality.

Below you can see how the major blues scale is formed. It consists of the first, second, flattened third, third, fifth, and sixth degrees of a major scale.

'C' Major Blues Scale

Degrees 1 – 2 – 3♭ – 3 – 5 – 6

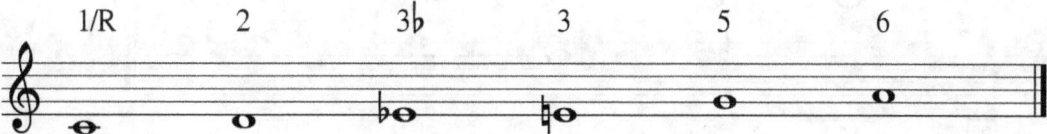

Another way of working out a scale rather than thinking in terms of degrees, is to think in terms of steps.

W – H – H – W+H – W

It is a good idea to practice over several octaves, start with one before practicing over two and then even three octaves, increasing it as you feel comfortable.

Major Blues Scale (Key Of 'C') Over Two Octaves

Key of A

Key of B♭
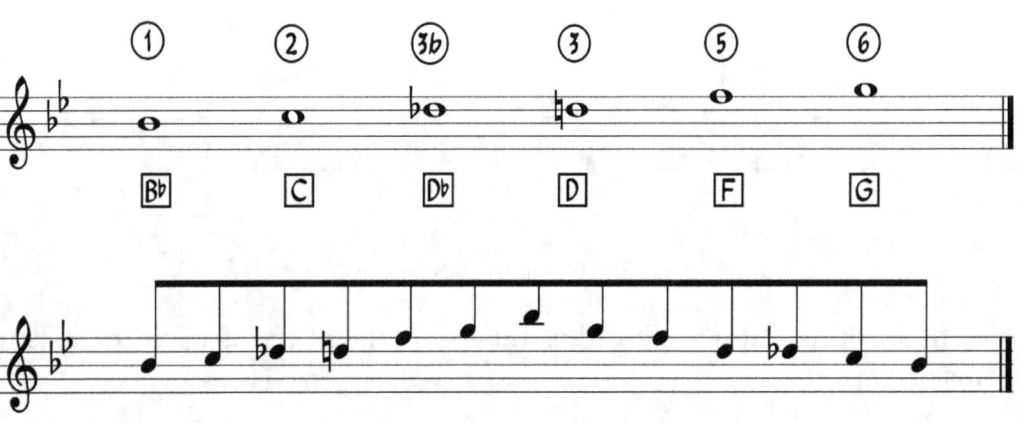

Key of B

Key of C

Key of D♭

Key of D

Key of E♭

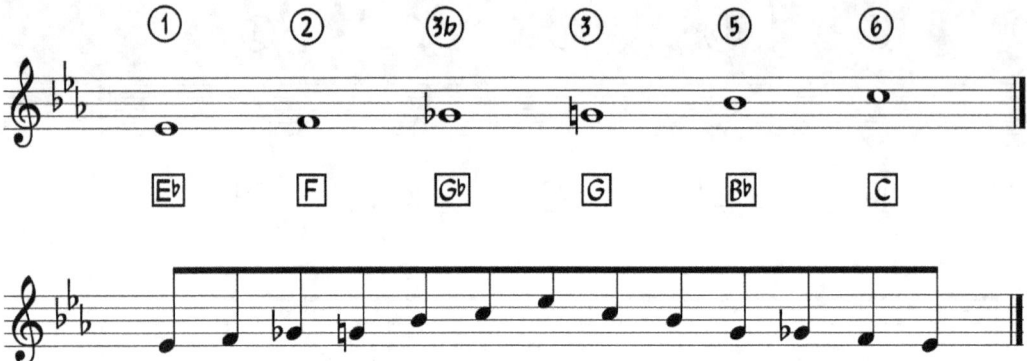

Key of E

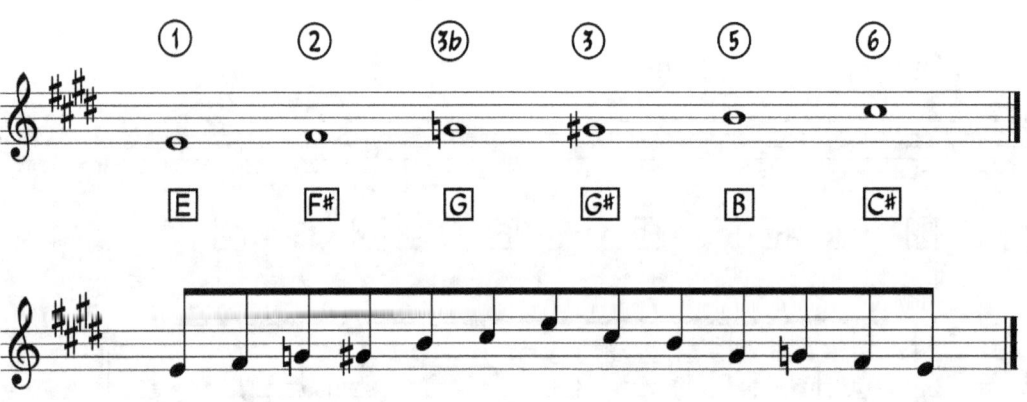

Key of F

Key of F♯

Key of G

Key of A♭

Once you know your major scales, how do you begin to use them in practice. The most obvious place to start is using them in their entirety, just running up and down the scale as it is formed. Use them individually or combine the two together, which helps to lessen the chance of sounding monotonous. Examples below are in the key of 'C'.

Major Pentatonic

Major Blues

Combined Pent / Blues

Bars four and five give an example of how you might incorporate a run within a blues piece using the major blues scale.

Another option is to create a broken run, that is one that switches around the notes rather than following the scale directly as it is formed. The combinations possible are beyond count, but here are a few to give some ideas of what is meant by this. Once you are fluent with the scales, creating something new is a case of experimenting with the notes available to you. These examples are all triplets, but experiment with all manner of timing ideas.

1.

2.

3.

4.

5.

Scales are the building blocks of music so the various riffs and licks that you learn will all evolve around one scale or another. This helps when learning a new riff as it will fall into a pattern within a scale or chord that can then be transposed to another key/chord. These examples are all created within the scope of the major pentatonic and major blues scales. You may notice that keeping strictly within only the one scale is very limiting.

1.

2.

3.

4.

A 12-bar blues example using only the major blues and pentatonic scales. Mostly single line melody with the occasional chord over a simple walking bass-line.

Minor Pentatonic Scale

The minor pentatonic scale is used in many forms of popular music, it is only five notes long, hence the term 'pentatonic'. The scale consists of the first, flattened third, fourth, fifth and flattened seventh degrees of a major scales.

'C' Minor Pentatonic Scale

Degrees   1 – 3♭ – 4 – 5 – 7♭

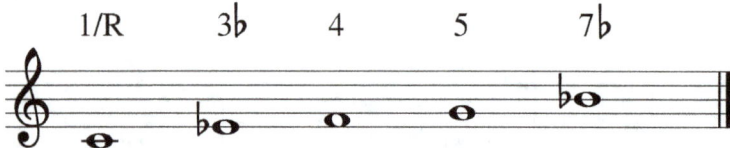

Another way of working out a scale rather than thinking in terms of degrees, is to think in terms of steps.

W+H – H – H – W+H

It is a good idea to practice over several octaves, start with one before practicing over two and then even three octaves, increasing it as you feel comfortable.

Minor Pentatonic Scale (Key Of 'C') Over Two Octaves

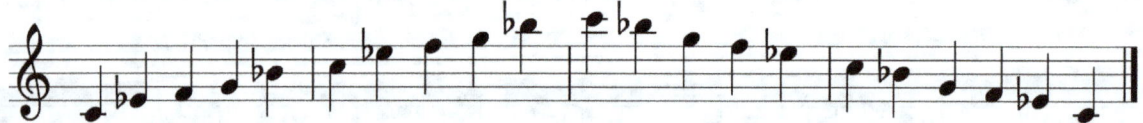

Key of A

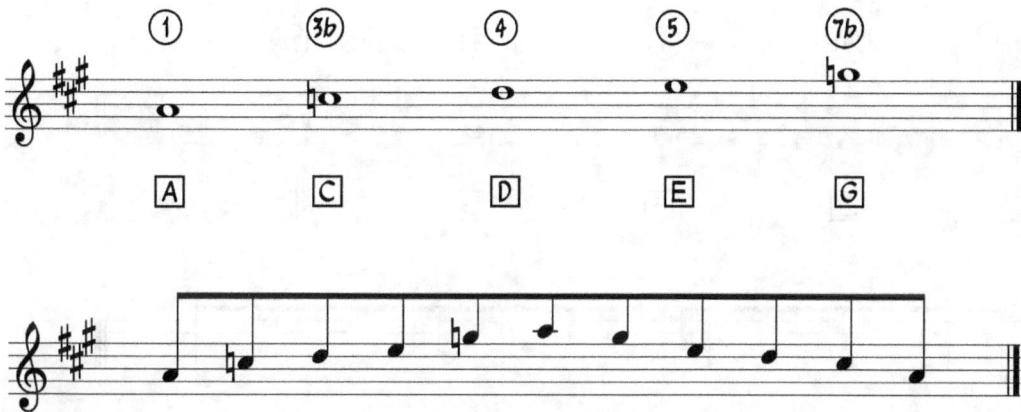

Key of B♭

Key of B

Key of C

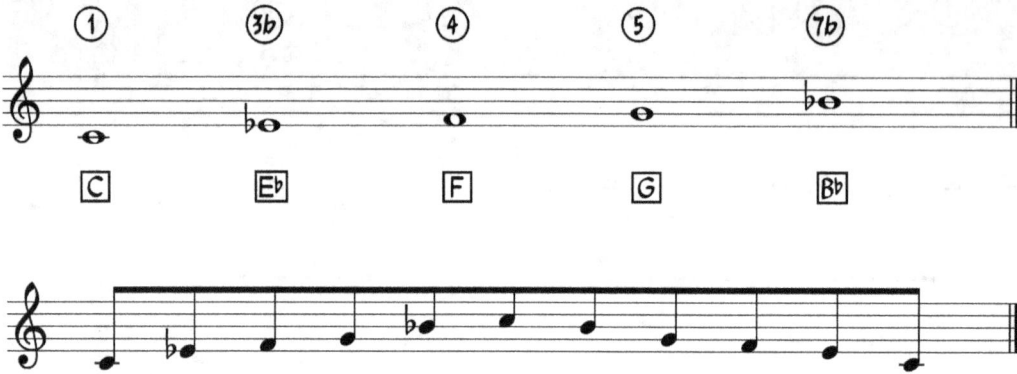

Key of D♭

Key of D

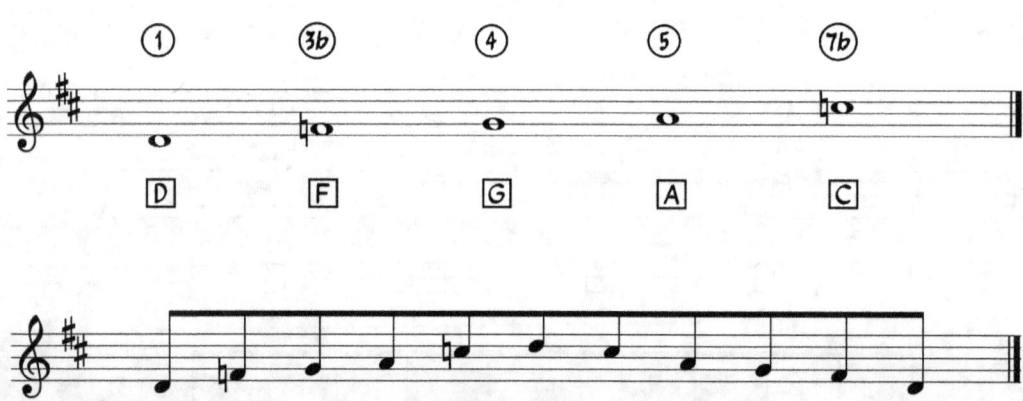

Key of E♭

Key of E

Key of F

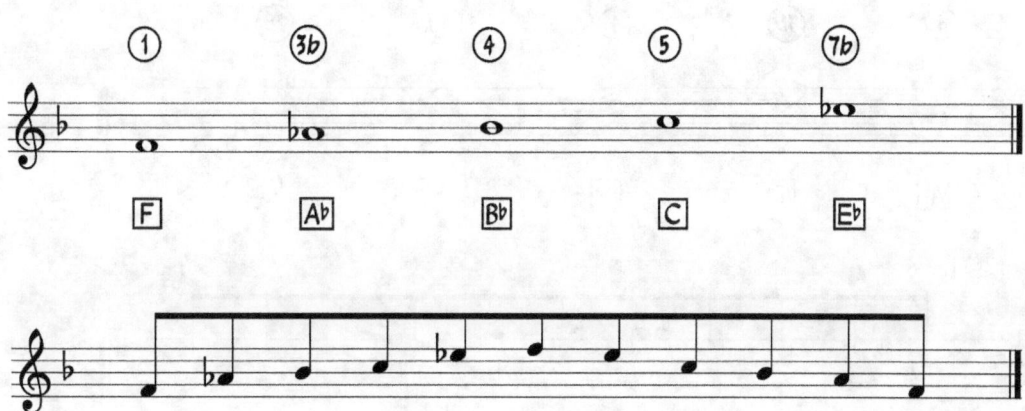

Key of F#

Key of G

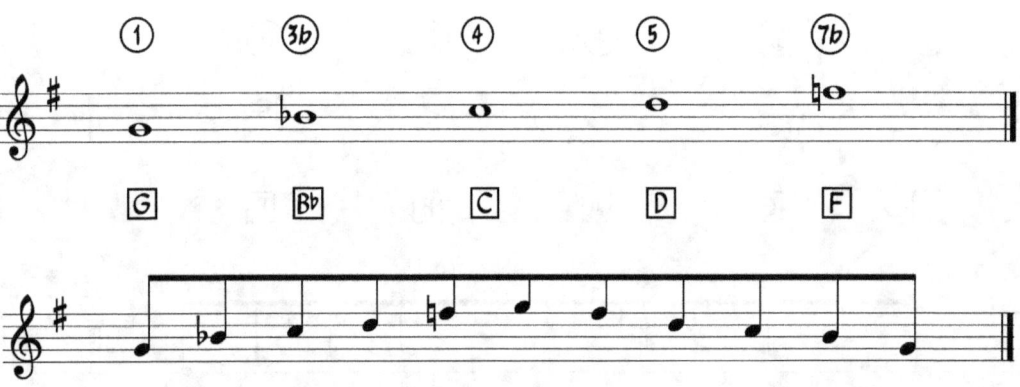

Key of A♭

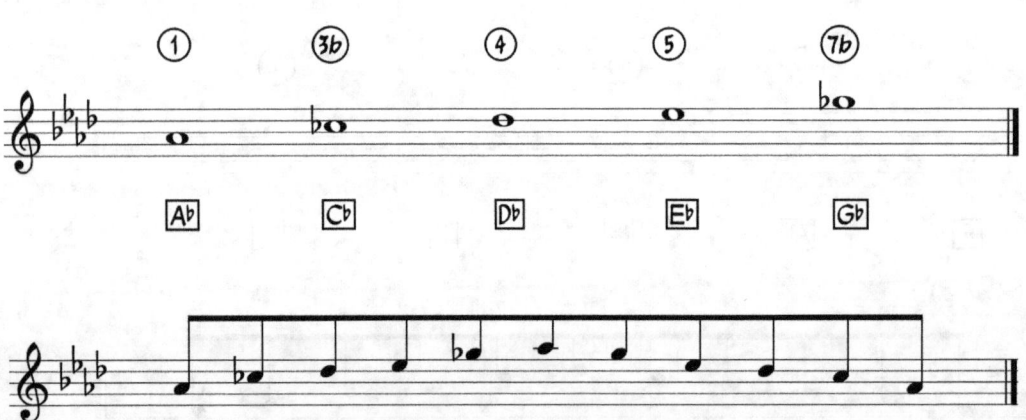

Minor Blues Scale

Perhaps the most definitive scale, being the one mostly associated with the blues. As with the major blues scale, in a strange sense it doesn't really exist, not in the literal sense of course, it's here, you can see and hear it, but at least according to traditional music theory it doesn't. This is because the minor blues scale is essentially the minor pentatonic scale but with the inclusion of an extra note (the flattened fifth) which is considered to be an alternative inflection. But for our purposes it very much does exist.

Below you can see how the minor blues scale is formed. It consists of the first, flattened third, fourth, flattened fifth, fifth and flattened seventh degrees of a major scale.

'C' Minor Blues Scale

Degrees 1 – 3♭ – 4 – 5♭ – 5 – 7♭

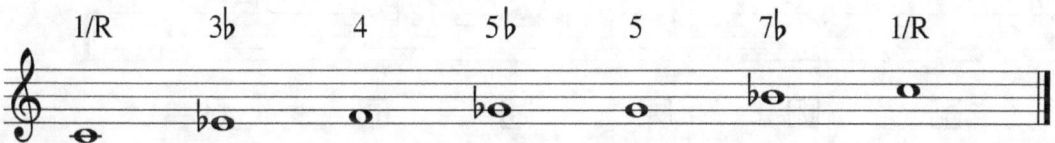

Another way of working out a scale rather than thinking in terms of degrees, is to think in terms of steps.

W+H – W – H – H – W+H – W

It is a good idea to practice over several octaves, start with one before practicing over two and then even three octaves, increasing it as you feel comfortable.

Minor Blues Scale (The Key Of 'C') Over Two Octaves

Key of A

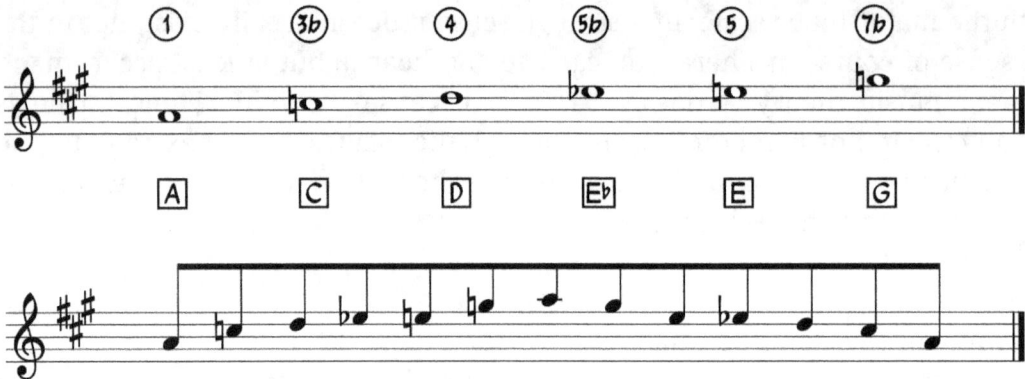

Key of B♭

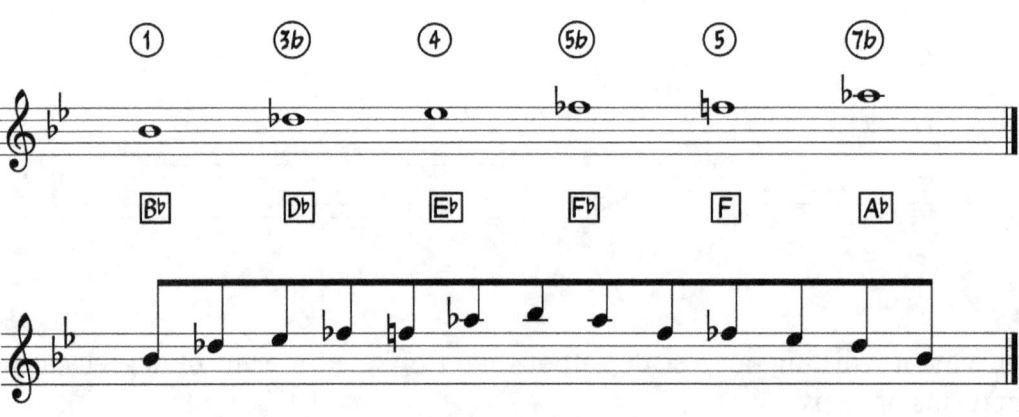

Key of B

Key of C

Key of D♭

Key of D

Key of E♭

Key of E

Key of F

Key of F#

Key of G

Key of A♭

Once you know your minor scales, how do you begin to use them in practice. The most obvious place to start is using them in their entirety, just running up and down the scale as it is formed. Use them individually, or combine the two together, which helps to lessen the chance of sounding monotonous. Examples below are in the key of 'C'.

Minor Pentatonic

Minor Blues

Combined Pent / Blues

Bars four and five give an example of how you might incorporate a run within a blues piece using the minor blues scale.

Another option is to create a broken run, that is one that switches around the notes rather than following the scale directly as it is formed. The combinations possible are beyond count, but here are a few to give some ideas of what is meant by this. Once you are fluent with the scales, creating something new is a case of experimenting with the notes available to you. These examples are all triplets, but experiment with all manner of timing ideas.

Scales are the building blocks of music, so the various riffs and licks that you learn will all evolve around one scale or another. This helps when learning a new riff as it will fall into a pattern within a scale or chord that can then be transfer to another key/chord. These examples are all created within the scope of the minor pentatonic and minor blues scales. You may notice that keeping strictly within only the one scale is very limiting.

1.

2.

3.

4.

A 12-bar blues example using only the minor blues and pentatonic scales. Mostly single line melody in the second half with a chord based riff in the first, both being played over a basic walking bass-line.

Relative Scales

Just as with the standard major and minor keys, the major pentatonic and major blues scales also have relative minors, which are perhaps obviously the minor pentatonic and minor blues scales. A relative minor scale uses exactly the same notes as the major scale it relates to, but has a different keynote (root note).

First let's take a quick look at the standard major scale and its relative minor. To find the relative minor of 'C' major, you look at the sixth degree of the scale (being 'A'), therefore, 'A' is the relative minor of 'C' major. Note how the two scales below use the same notes, they merely start with a different root note.

'C' Major Scale

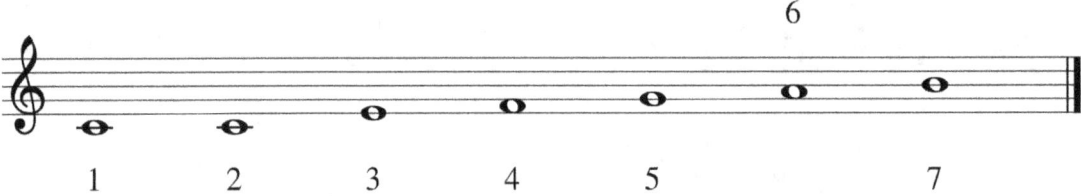

'A' Minor Scale

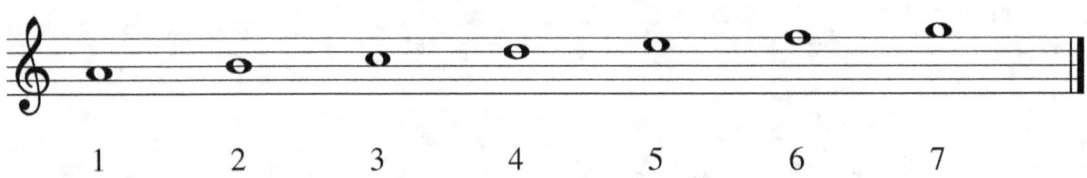

The pentatonic and blues scales follow the exact same rule as the standard major scales, with the same sixth degrees of the major scale dictating the relative minor of the pentatonic and blues scales. So the relative minor of the 'C' major blues scale is the 'A' minor blues scale.

> Some people don't acknowledge the major blues scale at all, they just see it as the 'minor' blues scale of a different key (indeed the minor scale often referred to as just the 'blues scale'). While this works to a degree, it's better to consider them as being the separate scales they are. It gives a more complete knowledge of the scales, which allows them to be better used and even combined when improvising.

The 'A' minor pentatonic scale is the relative minor of the 'C' major pentatonic and so the 'A' minor blues scale is also the relative minor of the 'C' major blues scale.

'C' Major Pentatonic

C – D – E – G – A

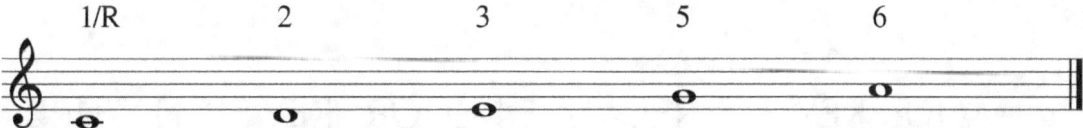

'A' Minor Pentatonic – Relative Minor To 'C' Major Pentatonic

A – C – D – E – G

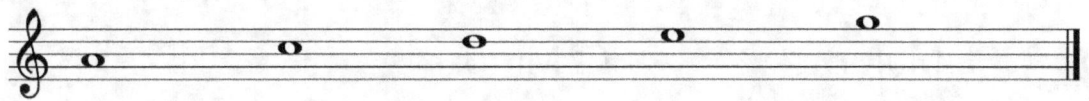

'C' Major Blues

C – D – E♭ – E – G – A

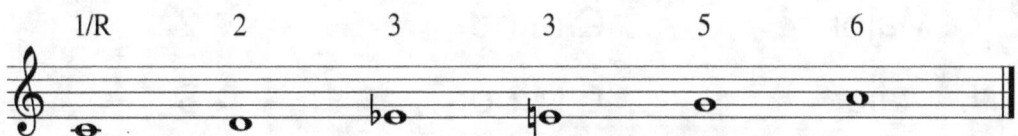

'A' Minor Blues – Relative Minor To 'C' Major Blues

A – C – D – E♭ – E – G

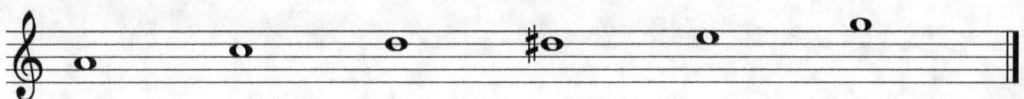

The chart shows the relative minor to all the major keys. Use this to help learn the scales that are relevant to you. It's important to always remember that as you learn a scale in a new key, you are also learning the scale of its relative major/minor key. This fact greatly reduces the number of scales that you actually have to learn with a kind of two for one deal, although the different root note can confuse matters when learning them initially.

MAJOR KEY	RELATIVE MINOR	KEY SIGNATURE
C Major	A Minor	0
G Major	E Minor	1♯
D Major	B Minor	2♯
A Major	F♯ Minor	3♯
E Major	C♯ Minor	4♯
B Major	G♯ Minor	5♯
F♯ Major	D♯ Minor	6♯
C♯ Major	A♯ Minor	7♯
F Major	D Minor	1♭
B♭ Major	G Minor	2♭
E♭ Major	C Minor	3♭
A♭ Major	F Minor	4♭
D♭ Major	B♭ Minor	5♭
G♭ Major	E♭ Minor	6♭
C♭ Major	A♭ Minor	7♭

Practicing Blues Scales

Once you know the scales, it helps to internalise them by practicing them using different methods. The first and most obvious is playing them as they are formed, up and then back down over several octaves.

Secondly, you can run through the scales, but starting on a different note each time really helps, as each pattern created feels quite different and requires much more thought and so helps you internalise the specific notes. The example below is based on the 'C' minor blues scale. The first starts on the root note, with each following example starting from the next interval up the scale.

1.

2.

3.

4.

5.

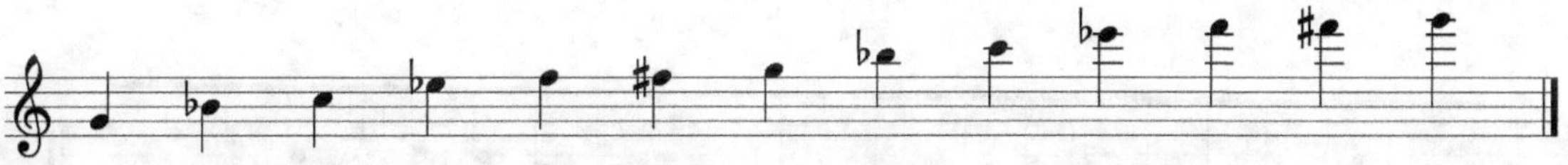

6.

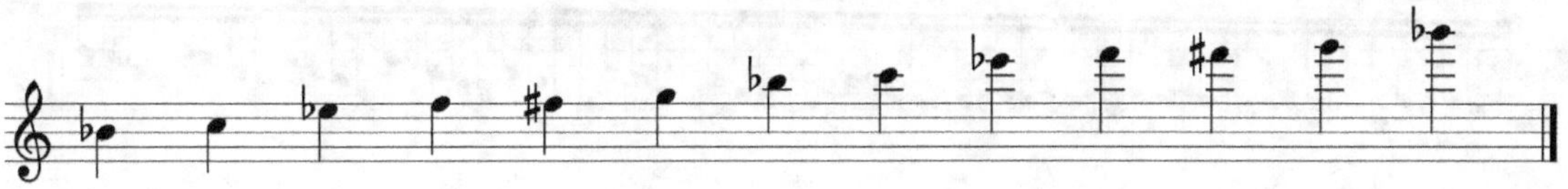

Another alternative way to practice the scales is to split them into smaller groups of three or four notes. Play each group one or even two of times, moving up each time so that you have started from each and every note of the scale. This helps as in reality you will use smaller sections of the scales when improvising rather than the scale in its entirety all the time. Examples shown use the 'C' minor blues scale.

Three Note Grouping

Four Note Grouping

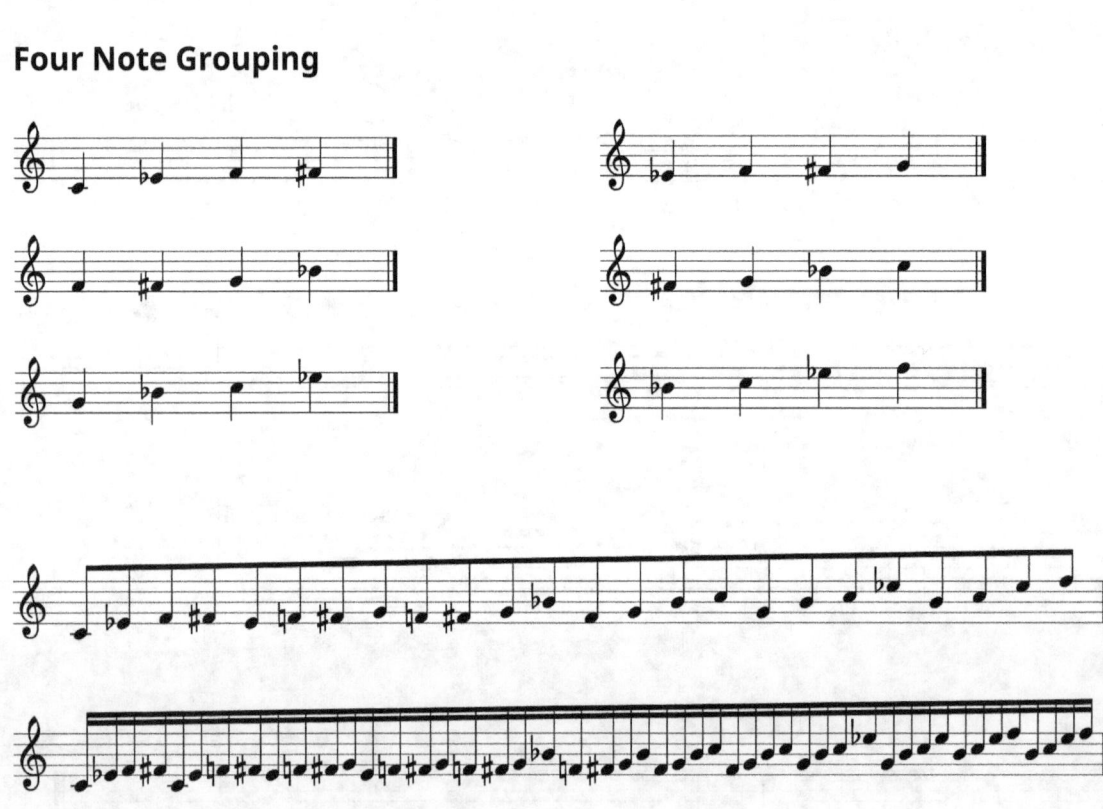

Combining Scales

While improvising try not to stick to just one scale, instead use combinations, switching from one to another. This is far less restricting and creates a more interesting sound that shouldn't become monotonous. The combinations are probably endless, but here are some ideas of what I mean.

This example runs up the major blues scale and then down the minor blues scale. You can hear how well they combine, flowing easily from one to the other.

Here you start with the major pentatonic, switching to the major blues scale when running back down.

The first bar uses the minor pentatonic scale, switching to the minor blues scale on the second bar.

Or alternately, don't simply switch from one to another, actually combine them together with the notes to both major and minor variations intermixed.

If you combine the major blues scale with the minor blues scale, these are the notes that you will have. Of course, this is not considered to be an actual scale of any sorts. If the blues scales themselves are not considered to be real (according to traditional theory) then this certainly isn't, but it is the notes that you might consider available to you. Example shown is in the key of 'C'.

The pretend scale above is only missing three notes from the twelve that exist, namely the ♭6th, major 7th and the ♭9th.

While these three notes do sound quite dissonant and out of place when played prominently by themselves, they can still be used as passing notes, particularly the ♭6th and the major 7th (major 7th perhaps used more in New Orleans styles). The ♭9th is more tricky to use and perhaps should be missed out, although a ♭9th chord could perhaps be used at a chord change set up, but even then cautiously.

Mixolydian Mode

You may or may not be familiar with modes, they are a complicated and involved subject that are used more by jazz musicians than perhaps any others. But here we need only skim over them to look at the Mixolydian mode. For a further in depth study of the subject, there are several publications to help you, but here is a very simplified run down.

A mode is basically a displaced scale, in that instead of starting from the root note, you start from a different degree of the scale. So instead of 'C' major running from 'C' to 'C' it could run from 'D' to 'D' or 'F' to 'F'. With a major scale consisting of seven notes, that means there are seven different modes, each with a name that stems from the old Greek modes.

The chart shows the name of each mode, the degree from which it stems and the resulting note intervals (T=Tone S=Semi-tone).

Mode	Major Scale Degree	Intervals
Ionian	I	T-T-s-T-T-s
Dorian	II	T-s-T-T-T-s-T
Phrygian	III	s-T-T-T-s-T-T
Lydian	IV	T-T-T-s-T-T-s
Mixolydian	V	T-T-s-T-T-s-T
Aeolian	VI	T-s-T-T-s-T-T
Locrian	VII	s-T-T-s-T-T-T

Mixolydian is based from the 5th degree of a major scale. If you take the 'C' major scale shown below you can see that in this case the 5th degree is a 'G'.

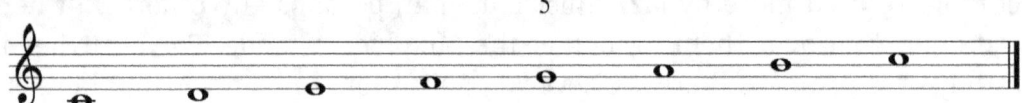

Below we now have the 'C' major scale starting from the 5th degree instead of the original root note. Notice that so far it consists of exactly the same notes as a standard 'C' major scale, just played in a different order.

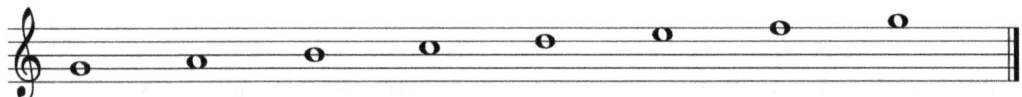

So far so simple, but what use is this to you? If you refer back to the chart again you can see the intervals that starting the 'C' major scale from the 5th degree creates. The intervals being T-T-s-T-T-s-T.

Tone / Tone / Semi-tone / Tone / Tone / Semi-tone / Tone

T – T – s – T – T – s – T

If you take these intervals and use them from the root note again, this is what you end up with, 'C' Mixolydian.

'C' Mixolydian

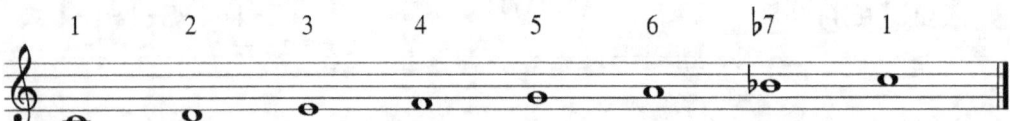

> Note that a simple way to remember this mode is that it is the same as the major scale but with the seventh flattened. If you look at the scale you can see that it contains the source notes of the dominant seventh chord 'C7', meaning that this mode works well over dominant seventh chords.

Key of A

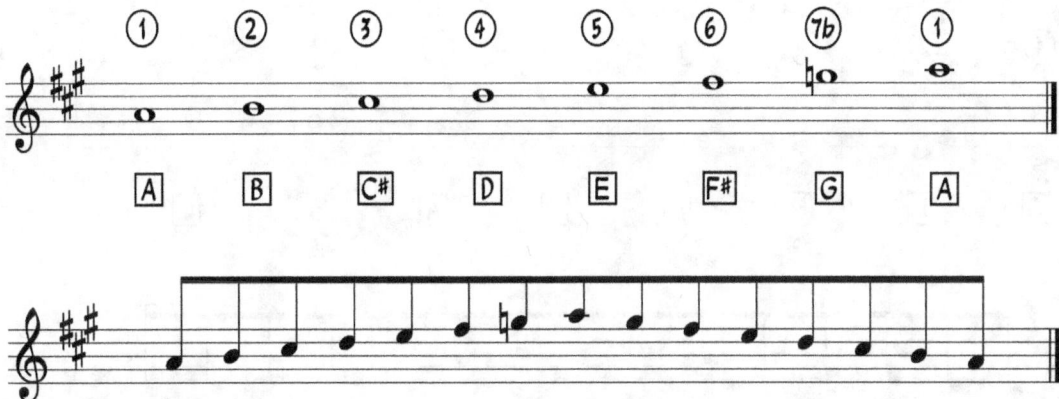

Key of B♭

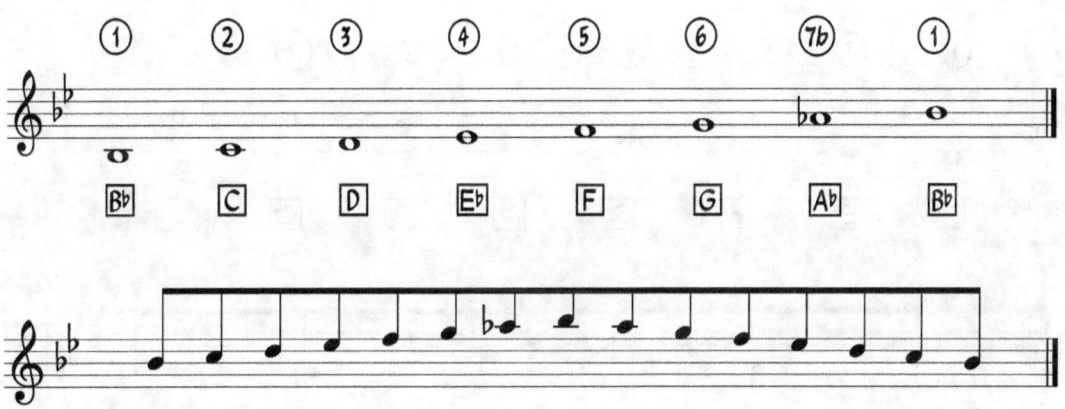

Key of B

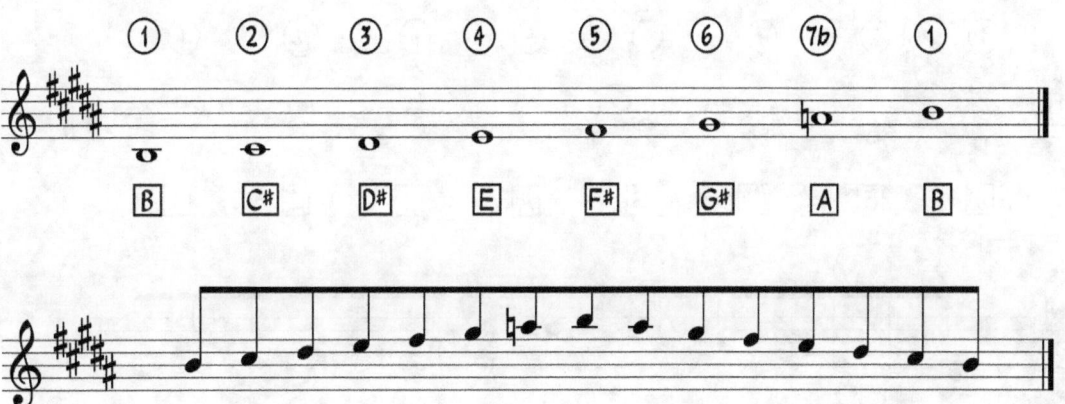

Key of C

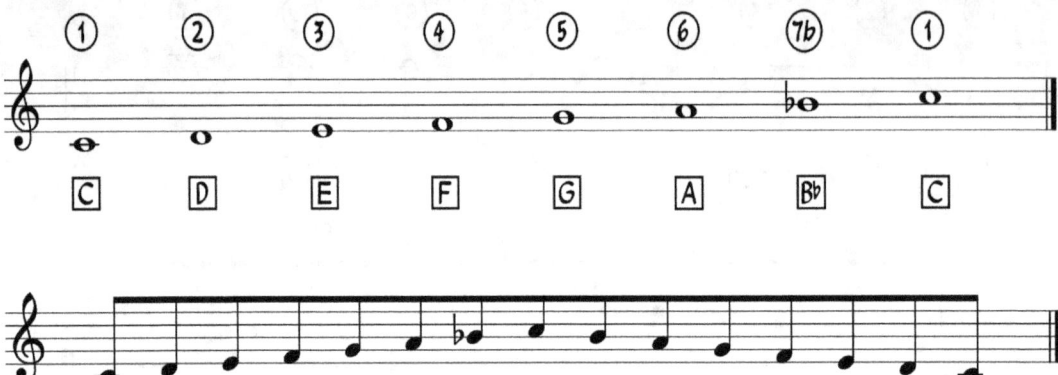

Key of D♭

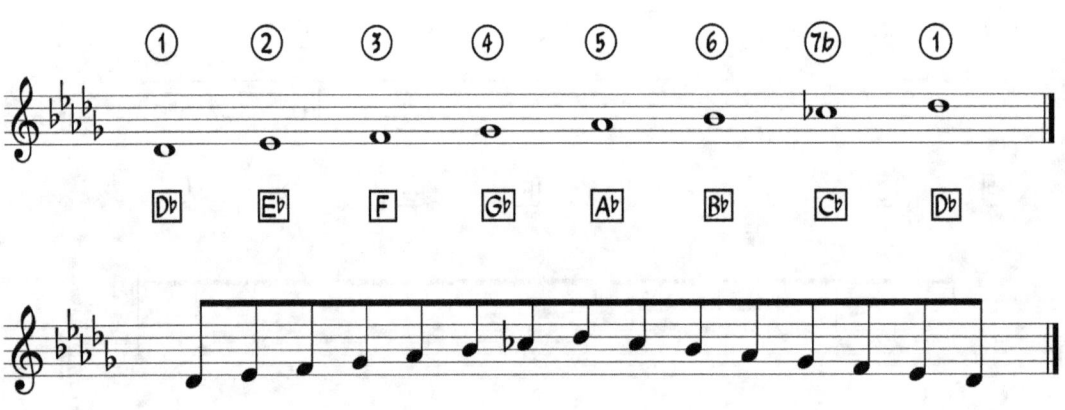

Key of D

Key of E♭

Key of E

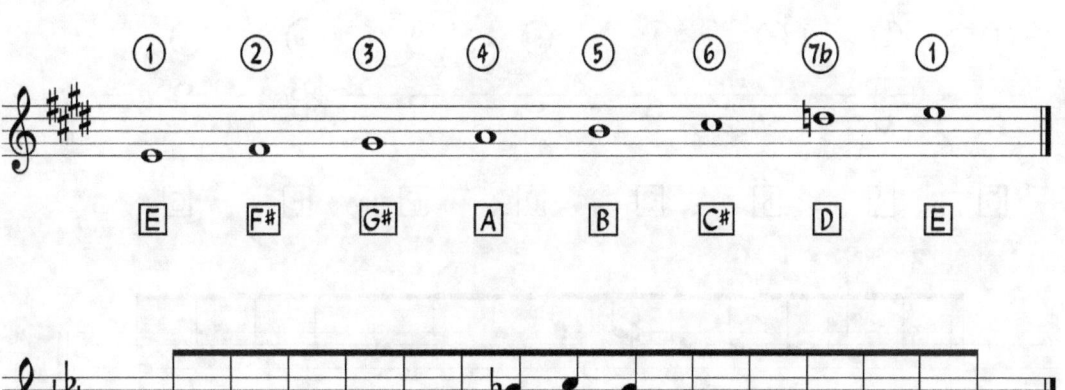

Key of F

Key of F♯

Key of G

Key of A♭

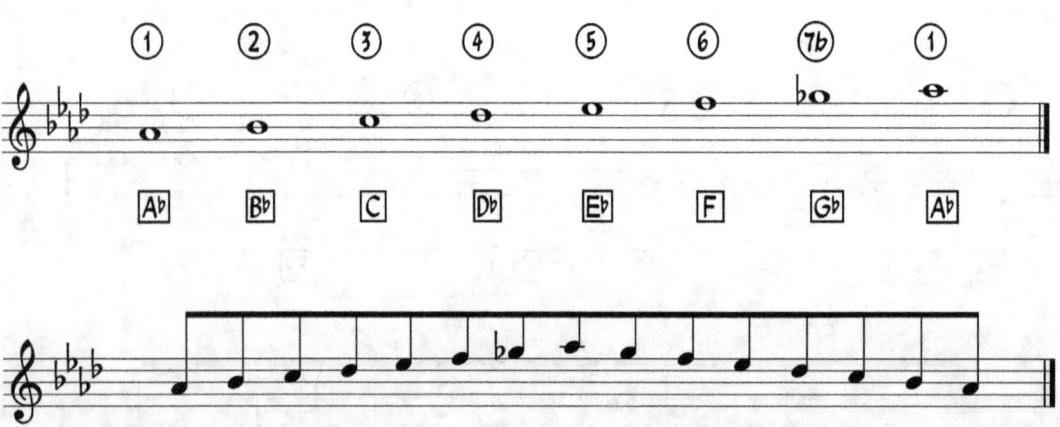

Mixolydian Mode

This 12-bar is an example of using the Mixolydian mode over dominant seventh chords within a blues setting. Notice that it creates a different sound to both the major and minor scales.

If we look at the triads that are created by building upon the Mixolydian scale, we can see that the chords are slightly different from those built upon the standard major scale.

Root Position

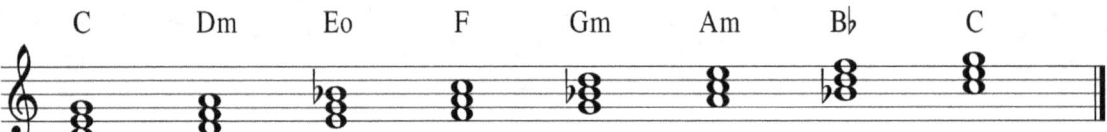

First Inversion

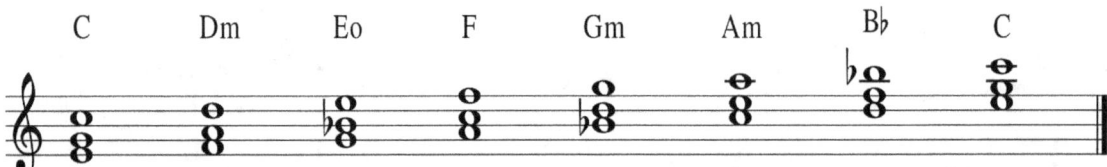

Second Inversion

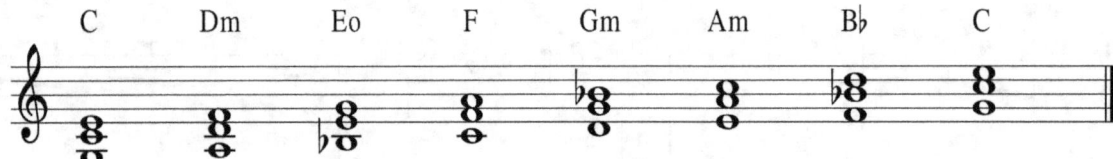

It is the second inversion of the chord that perhaps arguably sounds and works best. These are all to be used over a 'C' in the bass (shown below) with the slash chords indicating the chord being over a different bass note.

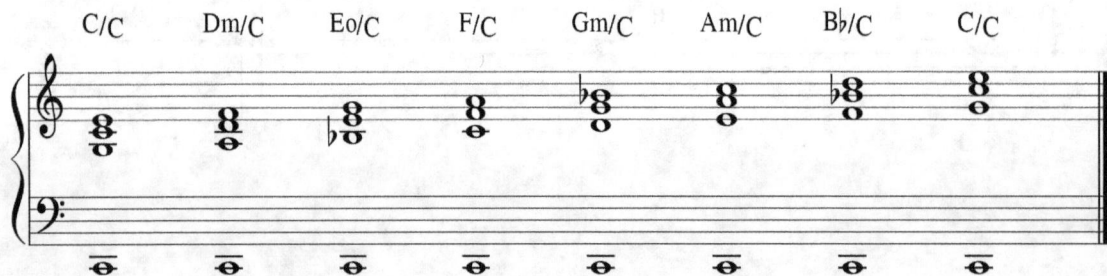

A few examples of how you might use these chords while comping over a blues based left-hand pattern. Some of these chords are obviously also formed within the major scale, but the flat seventh creates three different ones.

1.

2.

3.

Intervals - Thirds

An interval is simply the space between two notes. Thirds refer to an interval that stretches over three degrees of a major scale. The 'C' major scale below shows the interval between the 1st/root note and the 3rd degree, these two span across three degrees of the scale, hence the term thirds.

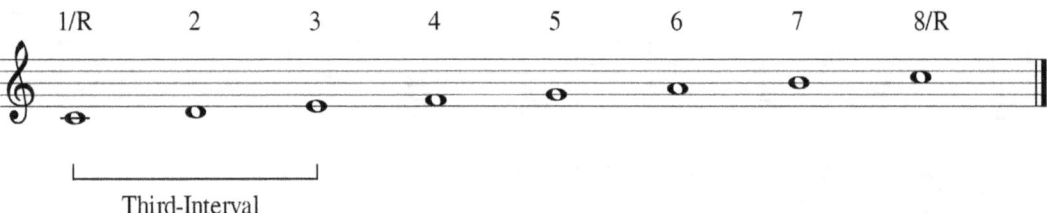

Below shows the third intervals available within the 'C' major scale. As you play through them, you will notice that they don't really create much of a blues sound.

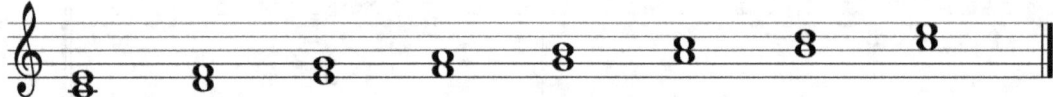

But that's fine as we can add to these with the inclusion of the third that's created from the diminished chord, the notes which are also the two 'blue notes' found individually within the major and minor blues scales.

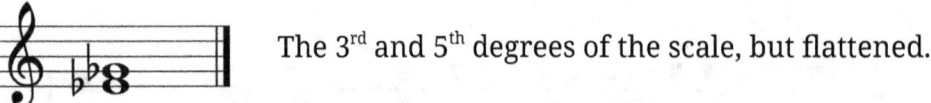

The 3rd and 5th degrees of the scale, but flattened.

The thirds created from the 'C' major scale with the addition of a third interval from a diminished chord below.

Even with the diminished thirds included we still don't have much of what you might call a 'blues' sound, so we will look again at the Mixolydian mode.

Below shows the third intervals created from the Mixolydian mode, the example here using 'C' Mixolydian.

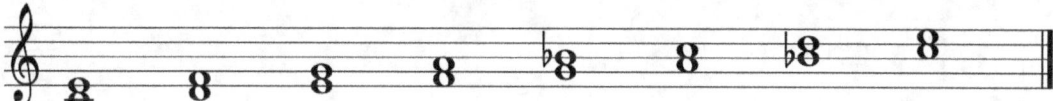

These can be combined with the diminished thirds to give you more options, as shown below.

The use of these thirds is a useful tool, with patterns consisting of only thirds or them being intermixed with other ideas. It is a good idea to get to know them well so their use doesn't require too much thought, allowing you to incorporate them easily into your improvisation/playing. I would suggest practicing them in each key over time until you have them committed to memory, as such they are included in the next pages. Some flat-thirds are notated as their en-harmonic equivalents to aid visual clarity, as otherwise it can become difficult to read, this is quite common in sheet music.

A

B♭

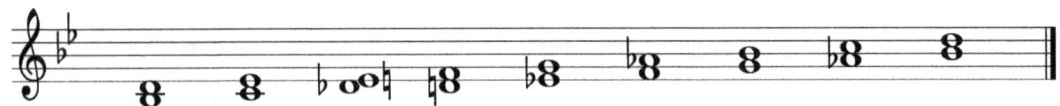

B

C

D♭

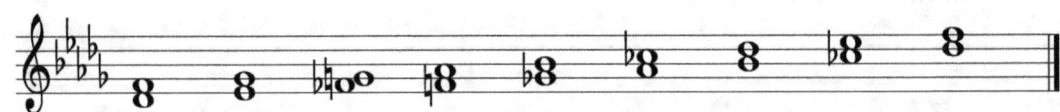

D

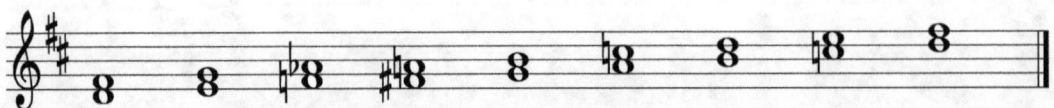

Eb

E

F

F#
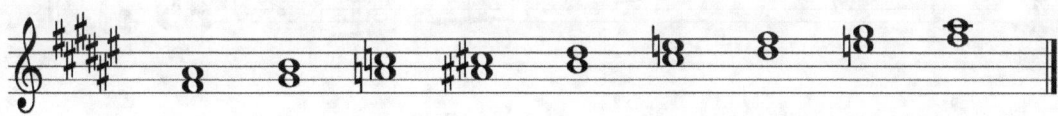

G

Ab

You can create patterns that consist only of thirds or alternatively combine them with other notes or chords. The possible riffs and licks could probably fill an encyclopedia, but here are a few examples to give you an idea.

Ex.1

Uses only thirds in a typical blues fashion, coming off from the diminished thirds (which are also the so called 'blue notes' the ♭3rd and ♭5th) which sound dissonant, to resolve up to the 3rd and 5th.

Ex.2

Here the thirds are used in a run down the keyboard spanning over two octaves.

Ex.3

Here the thirds employ the use of a tremolo in the first bar, an easy but effective technique. The tremolo asks a question, with the following short phrase then supplying the answer.

Ex.4

This third based pattern can be heard everywhere. This particular version alternates between the singular root note and the various thirds above it. The grace notes/slurs can be used to taste on both the 3rd and the 5th notes.

Ex.5

Continuous/repetitive thirds like below can be found in blues, boogie woogie and rock 'n' roll. Easy to play but effective.

Ex.6

This pattern uses a singular note intro, before alternating single notes and thirds.

The combinations of these patterns are near endless. It is best to take your knowledge of the available thirds and play around with them, using different combinations and timing, get a feel for using them. As you listen to blues music you will pick out sections that use thirds and copy them, this is really the best way to learn. Listen, copy, learn then create.

This 12-bar example employs the use of thirds throughout, intermixed with a few chords and single notes phrases. Once you have the idea/feel of it, start to create your own twelve bar improvisations using thirds.

Intervals - Sixths

A sixth interval is referring to two notes that are six intervals apart. If you look at the notes you will see that it is actually a third interval with its notes in reverse order. The example is in the key of 'C'.

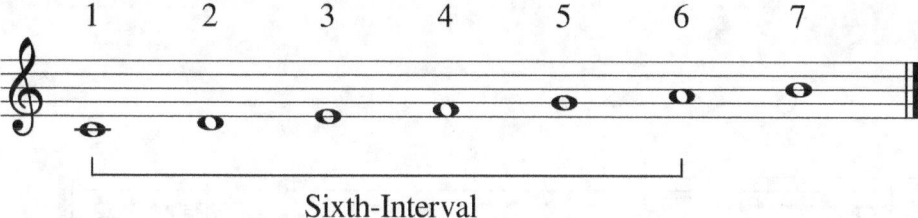

The 1st/root note ('C') and the 6th ('A') are six intervals apart, creating a sixth.

Sixth intervals in the key of 'C' following the Mixolydian mode, but also including the diminished sixths (♭3rd and ♭5th).

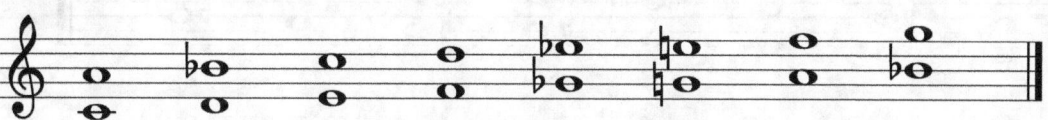

As you can see, the sixth intervals above use the same notes as the third intervals below, but in a reversed inversion.

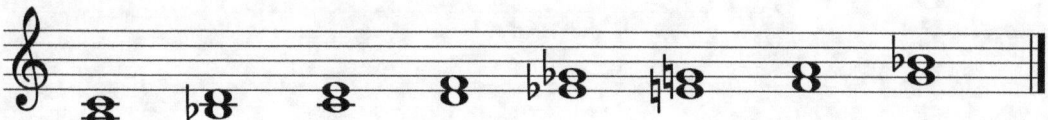

> As with the third intervals, it is a good idea to memorise them in each key as much as possible as this allows for much easier use while improvising. This will take time of course, so start on the key/keys you are initially practicing with.

A
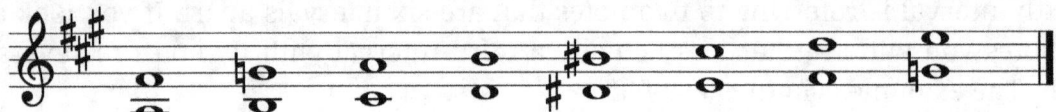

B♭

B

C
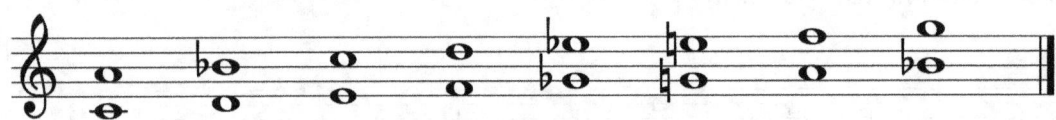

D♭
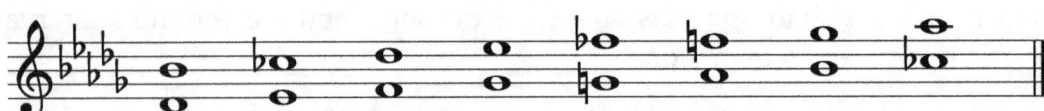

D
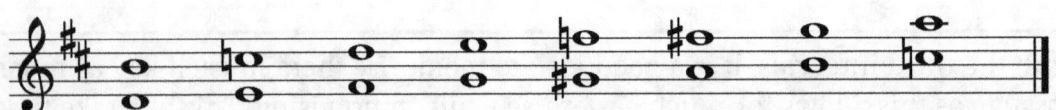

E♭

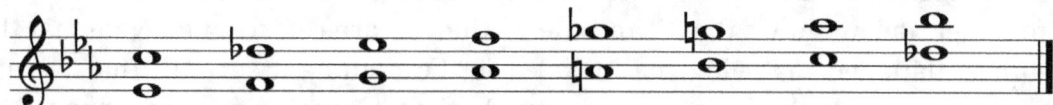

E

F

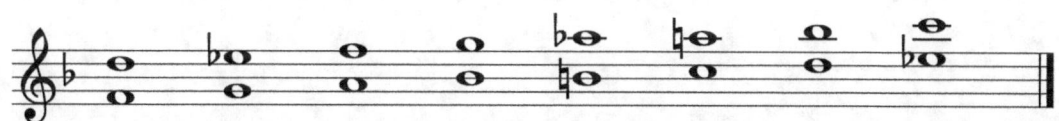

F♯

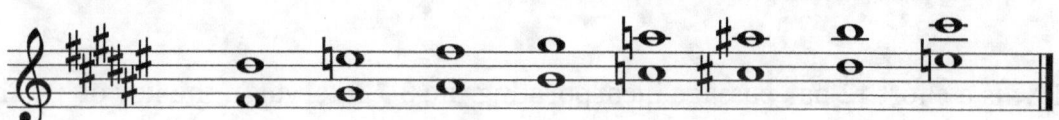

G

A♭

Intervals 3 - 7

Here we refer to a three-seven interval which is simply the use of the 3rd and the 7th together. Below shows the 3rd and the 7th that we are referring to. Note that the seventh is flattened (as being the blues) it is the dominant seventh that we are using. Also note that the scale used is actually the 'C' Mixolydian mode due to the inclusion of the dominant seventh.

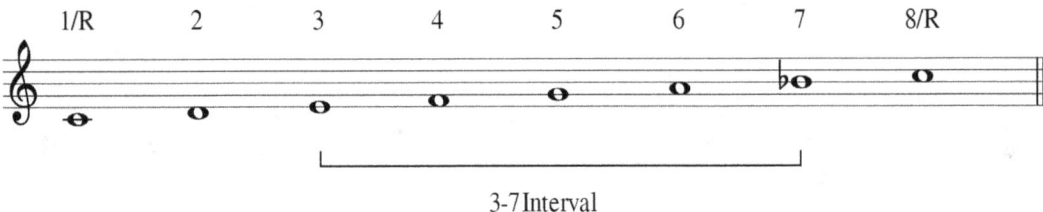

The three-seven interval can be played in two different inversions.

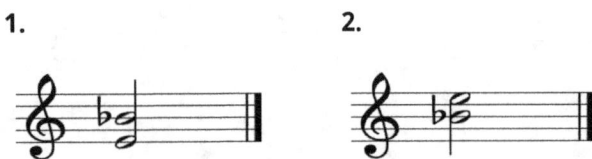

Below is a short 12-bar passage incorporating the 3-7 interval in the key of 'C'. The use of only the 3-7 intervals isn't very musical, but it is here merely to provide an example of them.

Grace Notes

An important tool in blues piano are grace notes, slurs, or slides (call them what you will). These are when you quickly slide off from one note to another note next to it.

It's believed that the idea of this stemmed from trying to emulate the way a guitar player can bend notes, or slide up/down the fret-board. Obviously on a piano this isn't an option, so blues players adopted the use of grace notes to create a similar kind of effect on the piano.

The example shows the 'E' being played with the D♯ as the preceding grace note.

The timing of these is unusual, in that the time value of the grace note is not counted. Both of the notes are played over the same duration as the main note (in this example the 'E' is worth one beat). The grace note is played extremely quickly, with next to no time value at all. You are just quickly skimming over it on your way to the actual destination/target note.

It is common practice to play these slurs by sliding the same finger from one key to the other. You ever so briefly strike the grace note as the finger slides down onto the main note. Some classical pianists may frown at this technique, but it is far quicker, smoother and more effective in this context. Bear in mind that the use of one finger isn't always possible, depending on which key you are playing in.

Use the second finger for both the D♯ and E.

The two most commonly used slides (grace notes) are the ♭3rd and the ♭5th, although the ♭6th can also be used at times, but not often, so for now lets concentrate on the 3rd and 5th.

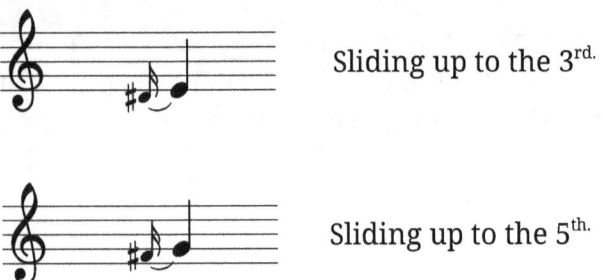

Sliding up to the 3rd.

Sliding up to the 5th.

With both these examples you will notice that you are coming off from a black key and down onto a white key. This makes sliding from one note to another a seamless process, accomplished best by using the same finger for both keys.

An important point to bear in mind though, is that this technique will not work in all keys so you will have to adopt a more traditional technique for other grace notes in certain keys.

Here we are in the key of 'F'. To slide up to the 5th you are now going from a white key to another white key, making the use of two different fingers necessary.

Here we are in the key of 'A'. To slide up to the 3rd you are now going from a white key to a black key, again making the use of two different fingers necessary.

Grace notes or slides can of course go in two different directions. The previous pages have shown the slide moving upwards (to a higher note) but you can also move down the keyboard too.

A notable difference when moving downwards, is that going from the ♭3rd or ♭5th you are no-longer landing on the 3rd and 5th (which are clean sounding) instead you will land on the 4th or 9th, both of which will sound a little dissonant. This of course is a useful tool when used correctly, but remember that these will be used more as passing notes that want to be resolved, so don't linger. Examples in the key of 'C'.

 Sliding down from the ♭3rd to the 2nd/9th.

 Sliding down from the ♭5th to the 4th.

Another option is to slide up to the 6th, from the ♭6th

 Sliding up from the ♭6th to the 6th.

Tremolos

A tremolo is similar to a trill, it is basically where two notes (or more) are played rapidly, fluttering alternately between themselves continuously for the duration shown. The difference between a trill and a tremolo is that a trill uses only two notes that are either a semi-tone or a whole-tone apart at the most, whereas a tremolo is far more varied and free. Any interval between notes is possible (if it sounds right of course) plus it can vary from just two notes to an entire chord.

The use of the trill/tremolo is extremely common within blues piano and can be heard dotted in-between parts here and there. Sometimes entire sections of music can consist of chords played in a tremolo fashion to great effect. You may have heard talk of old blues men of the past sat at the piano whose hands trembled over the keys like it was crying, well that's the kind of effect you're looking for.

Starting with only two notes, this is an example of how you might see it written in sheet music.

The 'C' and 'E' above are played alternately at a rapid pace for the duration shown, which in this case is the entire four beats of the bar. You will notice that when it is written in notation the timing value of the four beats isn't split between them (both notes being notated as being worth two beats each). This is because although one note is to the left and one to the right, both notes actually span the entire bar, so they are valued as being four beats each.

Taking the example on the previous page we will look more closely at what is being shown. The number of lines shown between the two notes are supposed denote the speed at which you play the tremolo. In this case, we are seeing three lines, so the notation is pointing you towards playing the notes as demisemiquavers.

So looking at the same tremolo again in Ex.1

Ex.1

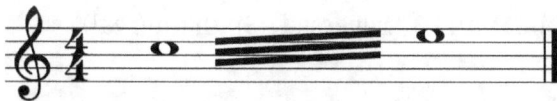

This is in essence, just a far more convenient way of writing what is shown below in Ex.2. It means the same thing, but creates a far tidier piece of notation on the page, and is also easier to read.

Ex.2

Now although it's shown written in full above, try not to think about them in such strict terms, it's merely to clarify how the tremolo is played. In reality, play the tremolo at roughly the right speed, but if the number of notes played (if they were counted) are one or two short of what is notated, it doesn't matter, these don't have to be exact as such (far from it) just fit in with the feel and timing of the piece.

The tremolo can be played in all manner of positions. Some examples based in the key of 'C' to show a few possible ideas of its use.

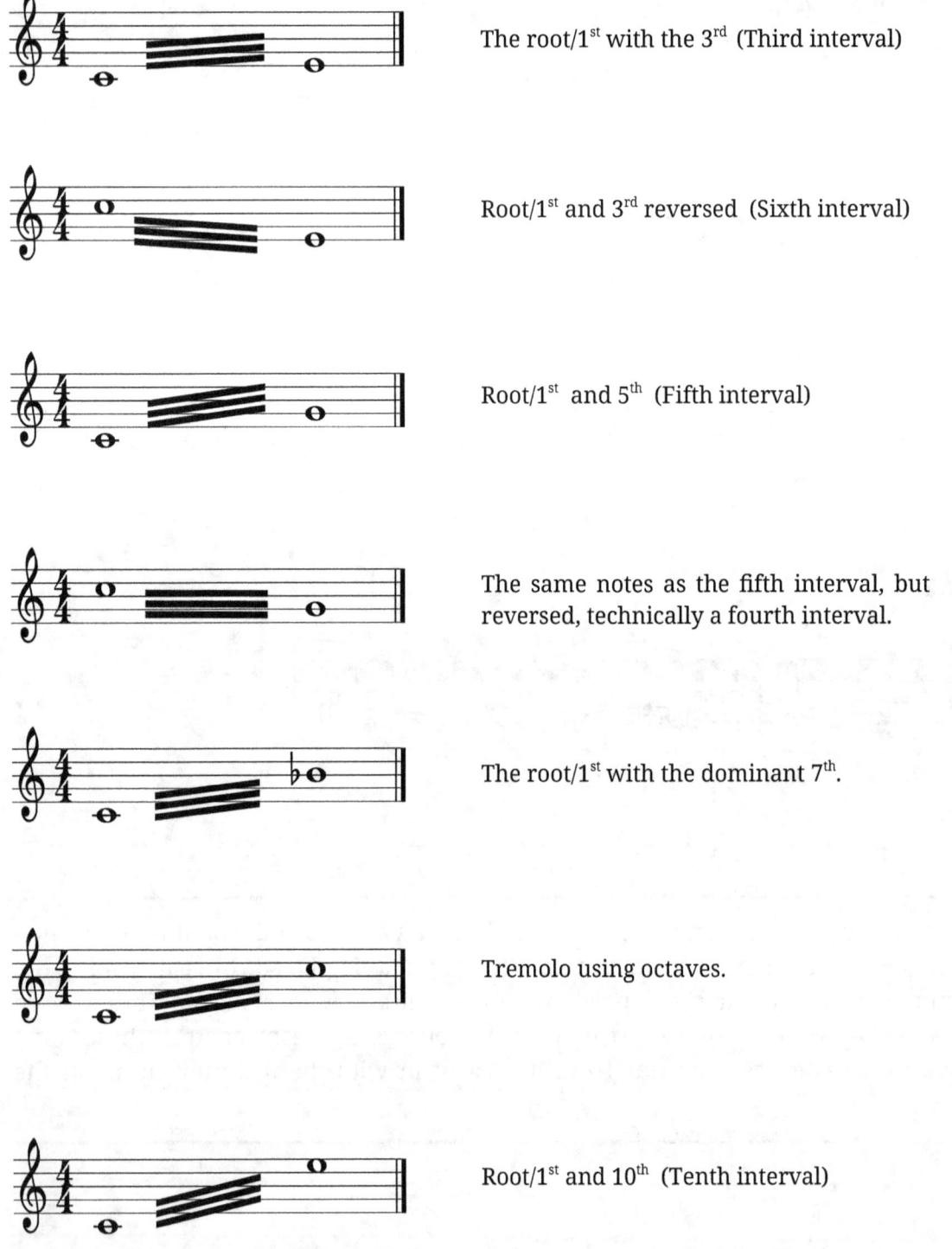

Perhaps a more common variation of the tremolo within blues piano can be found with the use of full chords. Whole sections of music can be covered just with chord based tremolos, varying the chords and their positions/inversions as you go.

A simple three note chord ('C' major) as a tremolo.

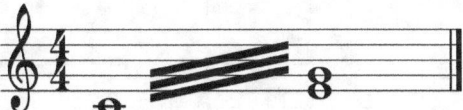 

'C' major diminished tremolo.

 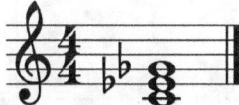

A four note chord tremolo ('C7'). The chord is normally split equally when notated.

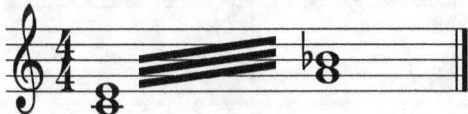 

A seven chord using only three notes. Omitting the fourth note, in this case the root note 'C' making this a rootless voicing.

 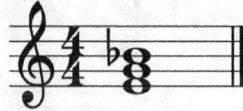

This short 12-bar example is to show some ideas of the possibilities when using tremolos within a blues piece.

Arpeggios

An arpeggio could be described as being a broken chord, that is a chord whose notes are played out separately, stretched over a certain duration. This can be as simple as the chord being played out once, or played over two or three octaves.

An example of a broken chord, each note stretched out separately.

The same chord played out over three octaves.

The arpeggio is a very useful tool for moving from one section to another, or simply filling in-between riffs, or as part of an actual riff itself. While you will see this sort of thing written out in full, you can also come across them written like the examples below. This is tidier on the page although perhaps not as precise or informative as when written out in full.

Or

You can of course repeat the same arpeggio over and over again and create something else again, a roll. Although you may well consider the arpeggio to be a short 'roll' itself.

Rolls/Rolling

What we are describing here as a 'roll' could be described as a fast arpeggio that repeats itself. Others may call this by another name, but it is a good description of the sound it creates, as the repeating pattern creates a sound that kind of rolls over itself, again and again. In some respects it produces an effect that isn't totally dissimilar to the tremolo in the way that it can fill in.

To create a 'roll' you can use a combination of notes from an appropriate scale, or just use the chords of that particular bar. There are so many potential variations of what you could do that we can't cover them all, but this will give you the idea. A 'roll' can consist of anywhere between three notes to five notes, although four is easier to play unless it contains a slide/grace note bringing it up to five, but with only four fingers required.

Below you can see the idea of what is played. This is based on the chord 'C6' starting from the top with the root and moving down to the third. As you can see it is just a simple arpeggio really, but repeated over and over again.

You can see that it's written with demisemiquavers (32nd notes) which is pretty typical, giving each beat here eight notes, or two repeats of the rolling chord.

Examples of different possibilities.

Four note roll using the chord 'Cm6' starting from the 5th.

Four note roll using the chord 'C7' starting from the root/1st.

Four note roll using the chord 'Cm7' starting from the root/1st.

Four note roll using the chord 'C9' starting from the 9th.

Here we have an example of a five note roll. You will notice that this is occupying the same space/duration as the four note roll, but each beat is now divided into ten notes instead of eight.

When playing this kind of thing you will probably find it easier to play two of the notes (in this case the 'B♭' and the 'A') with the same finger. To try to use all five fingers of your right-hand in this manner will feel awkward and possibly sound so. This sliding from one key to another is common place in blues piano and will eventually become natural to you, as well as helping to create that authentic sound.

Example of typical fingering

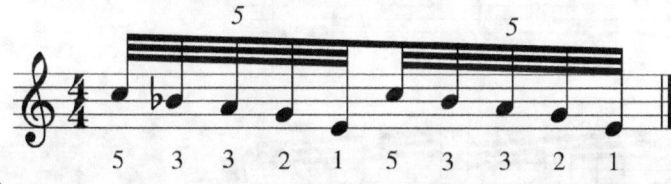

Examples so far have all created a downwards motion, but you also create them using an upward motion as well, although this isn't heard anywhere near as often.

Here you are using as the notes of a 'Cm9' chord. Beginning at the 9th, sliding from the ♭3rd to the 3rd with the same finger and finishing on the 7th.

Or a simpler three note pattern shown below. Here being formed from part of a 'C6' chord. Beginning on the 5th, using the 6th and ending on the root/1st. Each beat is divided into two sets of triplets, so each half beat is subject to the repeating three note triplet pattern.

Another trick is that you can play around with the timing/tempo of the rolls. Meaning that you can start off slowly, and then increase the speed, or vice versa, start fast and then slow the roll down before you move onto something different. Although the timing has been written out here to a fashion, when changing the speed of a 'roll' in reality, don't be strict with it like in the notated examples here, just do it by feel.

Example.1

Example.2

Here the transition is more gradual. Bar one has four repeats of the pattern, bar two has six repeats and bar three has eight repeats.

Example.3

Here you have the same four note pattern, starting off slowly, its speed increasing over bar two and settling down on bars three and four. The tempo is then slowed back down again over the course of the last two bars. You can also try using dynamics to accentuate the change, with the fast sections being a little louder compared to the slower sections being played softer.

Best tip with the 'rolls', is not to over think it too much, the examples might be written in full, but that's just to confirm what is being played. When you actually play them just play by feel rather than being hung-up on the exact timing somebody else has written down.

Take this bar below for instance, it shows you a 'roll' using the chord 'F9', but when improvising simplify your thought process. So although this might be what you actually play...

Don't think of it as being any more complicated than the simple chord shown below. Just instead of playing it in full, you're playing in a repeated downward arpeggio like fashion. Try not to think, just play.

All manner of possibilities exist, these are just a small selection to give you an idea of what you might use. Experiment around yourself using the chords in different inversions, omitting different notes or try using some of the different scales suitable for blues music, using combinations of different notes picked out from the scale. And above all else, listen to as much recorded music as you can, this will help you internalise the sound that you are looking for.

A 12-bar blues incorporating some of the elements we have just been looking over.

Drone Notes

The term 'drone note' refers to a note that is repeated or held above a riff/lick/phrase. The end result is a technique that is a classic part of blues piano playing. The examples here are in the key of 'C'.

You can see the constantly repeating note at the top 'C', this is the 'drone note'. The rest of the phrase alternates between two notes below, the $\flat 5^{th}$ and 5th.

The same phrase but the 'drone note' is now the dominant 7th over the same two notes below, the $\flat 5^{th}$ and 5th.

And here the 'drone note' is now the 5th, with the rest of the phrase alternating between the $\flat 3^{rd}$ and the 3rd.

Here we are back to the root note with the $\flat 5^{th}$ and 5th, but using a slight variation of the same pattern.

Note that these phrases all use the notes from the 'minor blues scale' and so when played from the 'I' chord they will work over all the chords of the 12-bar blues, 'I' 'IV' and 'V' chords.

You can of course take the use of 'drone notes' a little further and introduce their use into more involved phrases. The 'drone note' remains at the top, leaving you the rest of the scale to play with below it. You can of course have the occasional break from the 'drone note' if it fits with the phrase, there's no hard and fast rules here.

1.

2.

3.

4.

5.

6.

Cluster Notes

A cluster note is a term used for a group of notes where the interval between the bottom two is only a semi-tone apart. They are literally right on top of each other, hence where the term cluster comes from, as they are clustered together. The most commonly used notes for this are the ♭3rd with the 3rd, the ♭5th with the 5th, the 6th with the ♭7th and the 9th with the ♭3rd.

The ♭3rd - 3rd cluster

The 9th - ♭3rd cluster

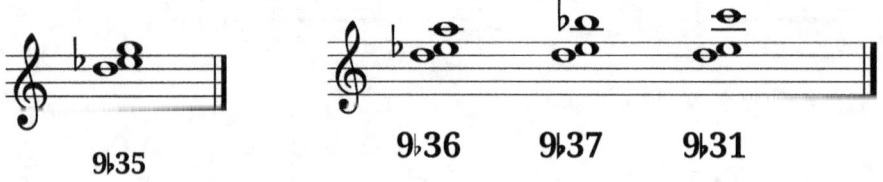

The ♭5th - 5th cluster

Blues Styles

Example Pieces

Boogie-Blues

We'll start with a look at a boogie type blues. Boogie-woogie is an off-shoot style of blues and much of it is related, including many of the left-hand bass patterns with this one being perhaps the most commonly used.

An example in 'C' of the common boogie type bass-line, sometimes referred to as the 'chop' or 'chopping' bass. It is created from the root note of the chord, with the 5th and 6th used alternately while played simultaneously with the root. Don't forget to play this with a swing/shuffle feel.

Fingering wise you have two options to try, personally I alternate between them a little bit (sometimes depending on the key) but try out what suits you best.

1.

Using your little finger on the root note with the thumb alternating between the 5th and 6th. Note that with this option your hand is positioned such that both fingers (5) and (4) can be placed over the root note. It is fine to use them both simultaneously on the same key as it reinforces it, but it depends on what you find comfortable.

2.

Using your little finger (5) on the root note, finger (2) on the fifth and the thumb (1) on the sixth.

There are many variations of the 'chopping' type boogie left-hand, learn as many as you can and remember that you can even vary the bass-line within the same piece.

1.

The basic 'chopping' type left-hand.

2.

Here the left-hand moves up to the 7th (dominant) on beat three.

3.

Here on the fourth beat you move down to play the $\flat$3rd followed by the 3$^{rd.}$

4.

Or combine the two together to create this version.

5.

This has the same ♭3rd/3rd part but now on the second beat, the last two notes are also altered slightly from the standard pattern.

6.

This replaces the root and 6th in parts with a single 3rd note.

7.

This replaces the root and 6th in on the last note only with single 3rd.

8.

Uses the ♭3rd and 3rd moving upwards, alternating with the root note.

These two 12-bar examples using the 'chopping' type left-hand boogie bass are in the key of 'C'. The first is the straight version, the second uses a combination of variations that you can alter as you feel suitable. It is highly recommended that you practice the left-hand separately, initially at least, because of the importance of left and right-hand independence. Practice this in as many keys as you can.

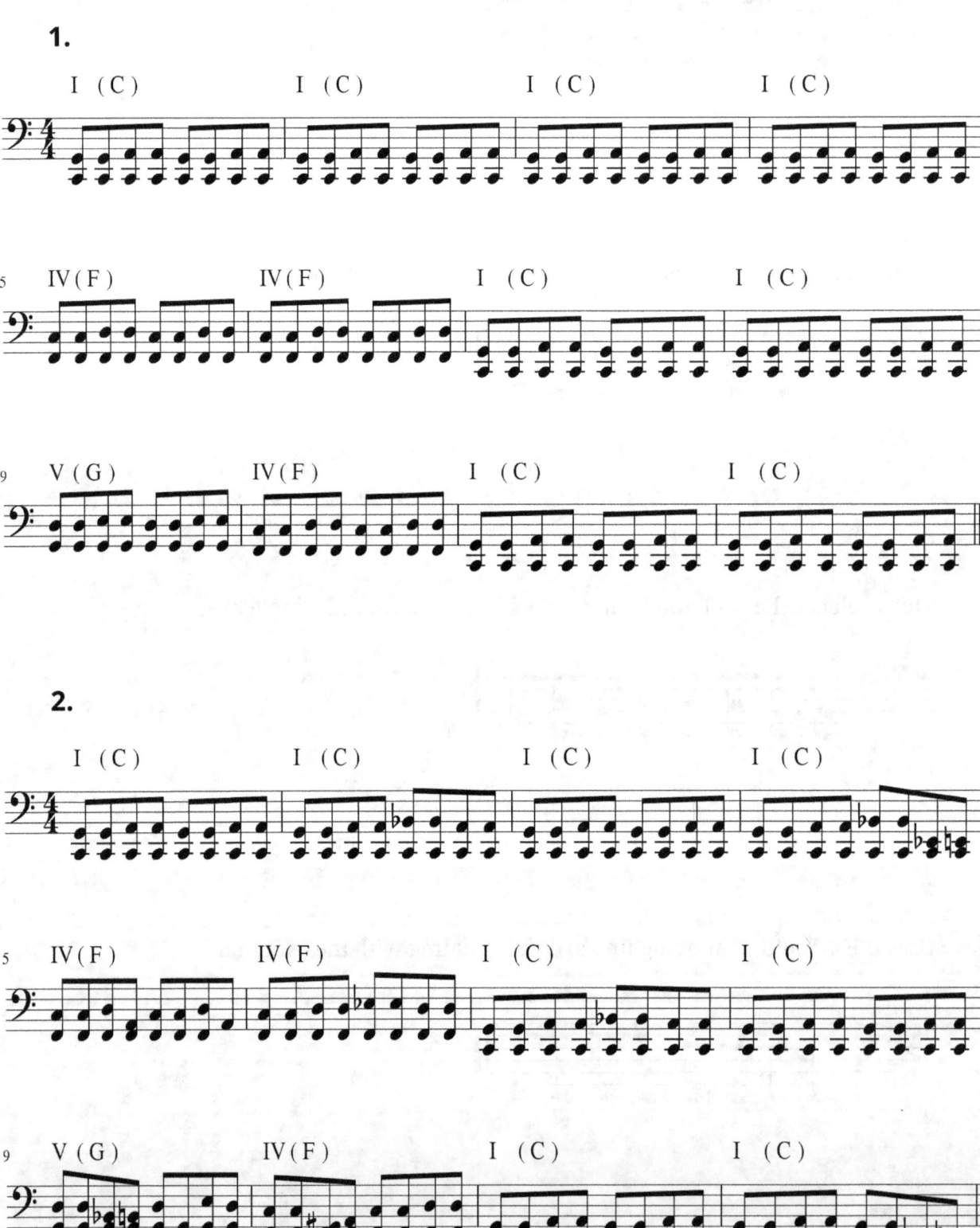

Boogie-Blues One

The following blues example uses a swing/shuffle feel, so remember not to play it exactly as written.

Sign denotes triple/shuffle timing.

This simple 12-bar employs the common 'chopping' type bass line, which stays the same throughout the piece, providing a solid driving foundation. Keeping the timing on the bass-line as tight as possible is important.

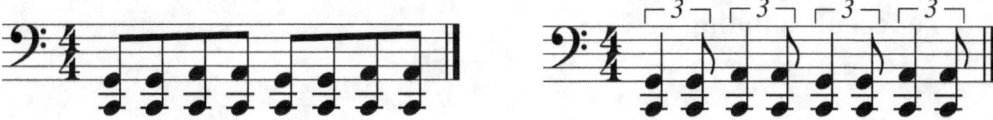

The right hand consists of only a few repeating elements. The first of which is this lick which uses thirds (intervals). The 3rd/5th moving up to the 4th/6th and then returning back down.

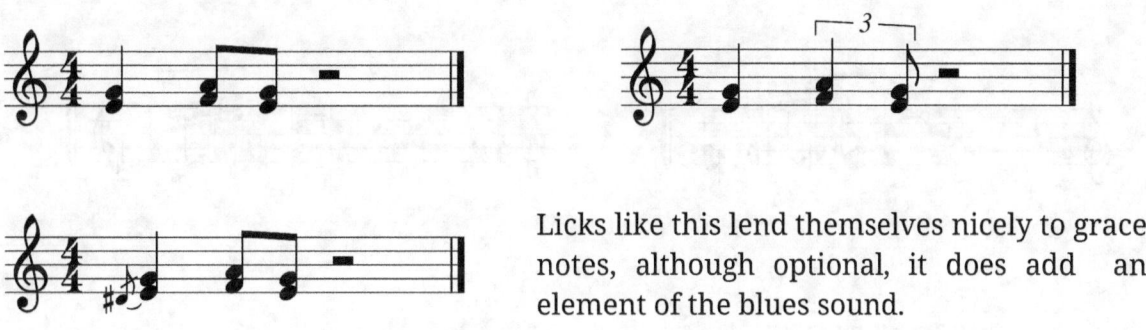

Licks like this lend themselves nicely to grace notes, although optional, it does add an element of the blues sound.

Note that when this changes to the 'IV' chord it flattens the third (Ex.1) instead of transposing the entire lick up to the different chord (Ex.2). The minor third of the 'I' chord is the same note as the 7th of the 'IV' chord, hence why it works so well.

1.   2.

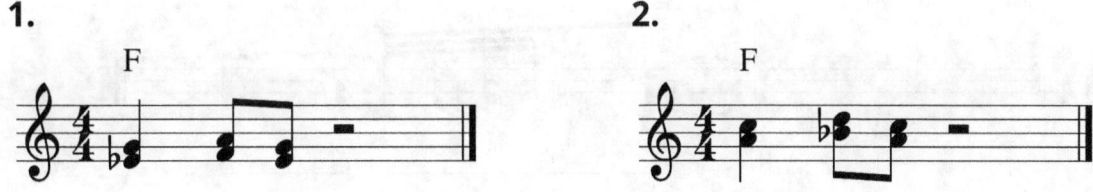

On bar 14 the main lick changes, but notice how it is similar? The timing has changed slightly, starting later, but it has the same movement of the 3rd to the 4th it's just that the thirds 4th/6th have been replaced with the root note one octave up.

Changing small aspects of a blues lick can create something new and fresh sounding. Even the simple act of playing the identical thing an octave higher or lower has the effect of sounding new.

There are two cross-over type licks used, the fingering numbers are shown but use what you feel comfortable with.

The timing on this second lick is perhaps more tricky so lets break it down a little. The third beat consists of a triplet (one beat divided into three) of which the first two measures are the 'F' and 'C' that are held over from the previous beat. This leaves one measure of the triplet (a third of a beat) which has been divided into four to create a fast little run downwards.

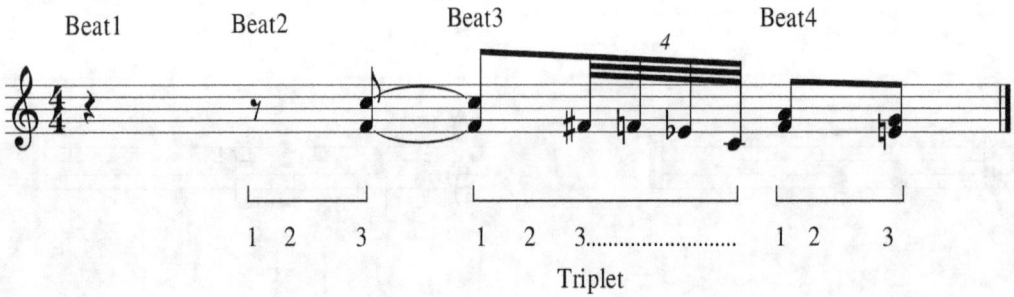

Boogie-Blues One

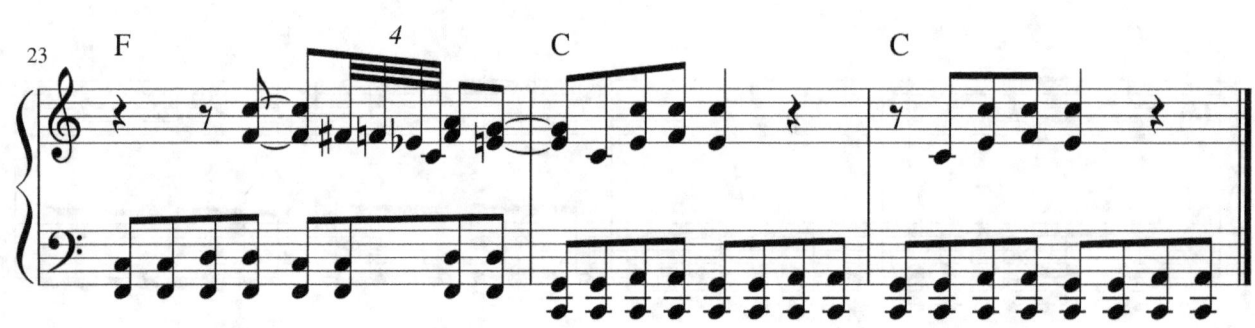

128

Boogie-Blues Two

 Sign denotes triple/shuffle timing.

The following example consists predominantly of a simple comping riff which starts as the root note played as octaves.

The same rhythm of this riff can be used to comp in many ways, starting on bar 13 the riff has changed from just octaves by adding the 5th in-between, which guitarists sometimes refer to as a power chord.

When playing a comping rhythm you can break up any monotony by occasionally adding a little something. Here we slide from the minor 3rd to the 3rd and then finish back up to the root note. Simple but an intrinsic part of the blues sound.

Or in the second half a slight variation on the same idea with the root note added to the 3rd and the following root note (octaves).

Boogie-Blues Two

Boogie-Blues Three

Notice in this example piece the first syncopated note on the first bar that leads into the main riff. Syncopated rhythms and this form of suspension (carrying over from the previous bar or beat) are commonly employed.

This riff uses a sixth interval which is really just a third interval (root/1st and 3rd) but in a reversed position (3rd at the bottom instead of the root/1st). The first beat uses a short semi-quaver following on to the 3rd interchanging with the 4th, slide notes can be used on the 3rd as you feel fitting.

In this instance on the 'IV' chord the riff has been transposed to the 'F', rather than being altered in any way.

On the second twelve bar sequence, the riff is altered so that it now continues moving upwards from the 3rd, through the 4th and onto the 5th. Small alterations to riffs can be used to easily create something new.

A simple pattern, alternating between the root and a series of thirds.

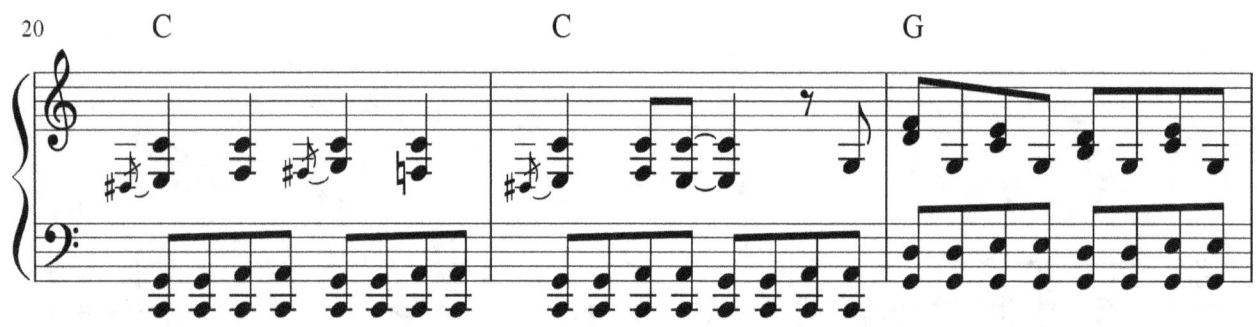

Boogie-Blues Four

This example piece uses a variation of the 'chopping' type bass-line. Instead of repeating the same 1st/5th to 1st/6th pattern, on the second measure of beats two and three it now changes to a single 3rd note.

The single bar intro uses a fast four note run that is also repeated throughout the piece. The timing shown in Ex.1 divides the last beat (beat four) into six measures, of which only the last four are utilized. Alternatively it could be written as Ex.2.

1. **2.**

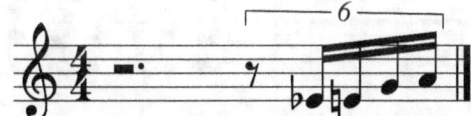 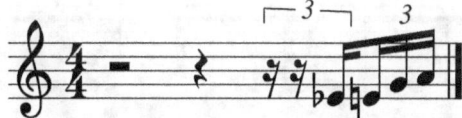

To help with the timing of this, below has the left-hand and right-hand both displayed in the same form. Although it's probably best to play this by feel rather than get hung up on the exact timing.

Bar 10 uses a triplet pattern, typically using the ♭3rd, the 3rd and the 5th. The bottom note here (the 5th) is held throughout in this case, although this could be omitted or instead repeated on each beat.

Boogie-Blues Four

Boogie-Blues Five

Note that this example boogie-blues is written using dotted quavers and semi-quavers to denote the swing/shuffle feel. Remember that the dotted-quaver/semi-quavers in example No.1 are actually played like the triplets in example No.2.

1.   **2.**

Looking at bars 2 and 3, it shows a very typical pattern that is used a lot, along with many variations that move around it. Using two different thirds that alternate with the root note. These are the 3rd and the 5th, followed by the 4th and 6th. Play these separately from each other along with the root note on the left-hand. You will hear how the 4th and 5th sound a little dissonant by comparison, which works so well when it's constantly resolving back to the more comfortable 3rd and 5th.

On bars 4 and 5 you can see a common variation of this which also includes the use of the dominant 7th.

On bars 6 and 7 you can see another riff on the 'F' that utilizes the exact same notes, being the root/1st, 3rd, 4th, 5th, 7th.

The thirds below are created from the Mixolydian mode with the additional thirds from the diminished chord. These are the building blocks for the previous couple of riffs we've looked at. There are many possible riffs/licks that you can create from these thirds, learn as many as possible and then experiment by creating your own.

On bars 13 and 14 you can see this riff again created from the thirds from the Mixolydian mode. Note the use of grace/slide notes here, using both the flattened 3rd and the flattened 5th. The amount of these used is up to the individual.

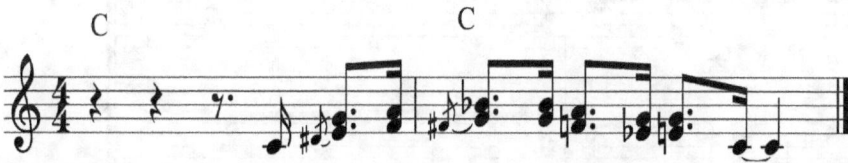

Here you have a riff on the first bar that is repeated on the second, but shortened ever so slightly. This is something you can do a lot when improvising, taking one thing and adding/removing a section to create something new.

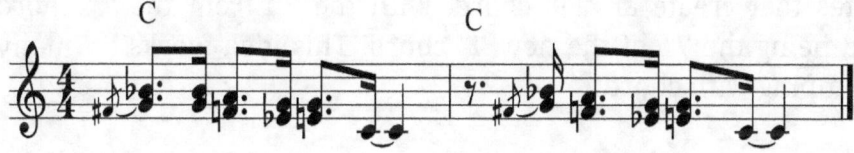

Bar 23, here a full chord as been added in-between all the thirds.

On some chord changes you simply carry the exact same pattern over, just transposed over to the next chord (shown below). Taken from bars 9 and 10.

There is another option to transposing the same riff, but this only works when changing from the 'I' chord to the 'IV' chord. Below shows the same pattern on the 'I' chord being transposed up to the 'IV' chord on the second bar.

But instead of transposing the right-hand up to the 'F' for the 'IV' chord we can make a small alteration instead. Keep the right-hand exactly the same apart from the 3rd being flattened. This simple change requires very little physical movement and utilizes the notes that create an 'F9' chord, with the 3rd from the 'C' chord you've just flattened being the 7th of the new 'F' chord. This idea works on many riffs, or when just comping with chords.

On bars 26 and 27 there is an example of this 'I' to 'IV' change by lowering the 3rd. The first bar uses thirds on the first two measures, but the same applies, only the 3rd from the 'C' is flattened to alter the riff to work over the 'F' chord.

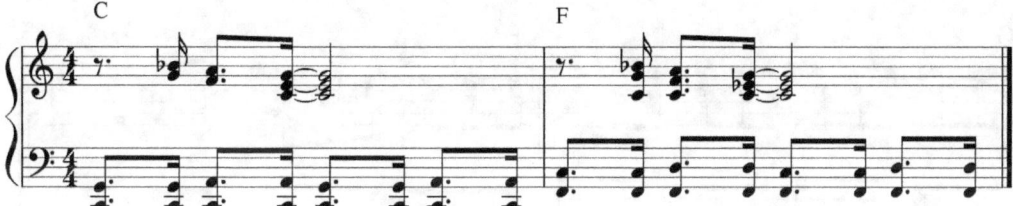

On bar 22 there is an example of the use of triplets, here in a continuous repeating three note pattern.

Note that the flattened 3rd is in use again, with the pattern starting on the flattened 3rd and moving straight to the major 3rd. The intervals used are stepping upwards 1) semi-tone 2) tone and half.

This same sort of pattern can be used in many positions, such as starting from the flattened 5th and moving through the 5th and 7th.

Or here, starting on the major 7th, passing through the root and finishing on the flattened 3rd.

On bar 34 you have an example of what is referred to as 'drone' notes (see section on drone notes). The triplet based pattern has the repetitive root note at the top along with the ♭5th and 5th alternating below it.

On bars 13 and 25 you have a simple turnaround that occupies only one bar compared to many that are spread out over two. Consisting of only two simple chords 'C' major and 'G' major, the left-hand walks-up to the 'G' using the 4th and ♭5th (still in 'C') both a semi-tone step upwards to reach the 'G'.

Boogie-Blues Five

Turnarounds

A turnaround is an important aspect of the blues, it takes place on the last two bars of the progression (on a 12-bar, numbers 11 and 12) rounding off the verse and setting up for the next one. The ending on a blues also incorporates the last two bars, but when ending you are moving to the 'I' chord whereas with a turnaround you are moving towards the 'V' chord. There are many turnarounds, here we look at a few simple ones and the classic blues turnaround. Personally I wouldn't get too hung up about the actual chords, just commit the patterns to memory and forget them.

1.

2.

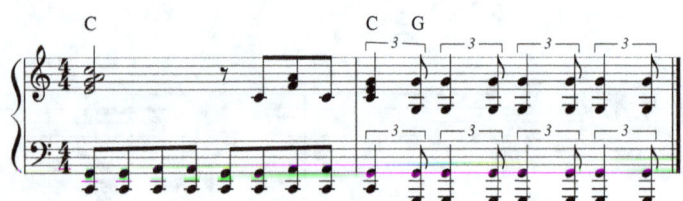

3.

4.

G♭

G

A♭

A

B♭

B

Crossover Lick

The crossover or x-over lick is an important part of blues piano. This right-hand lick is often being referred to as being the 'Dr John lick' as he was well known for its use, or just the 'famous lick' as its use is so common. I believe it is called a crossover lick as the upper fingers of the right-hand 'crossover' the thumb on their way down. That said, I myself don't always do this, as often you can also just drop the thumb down, but whatever works for you is fine. There are of course many versions of this type of thing, here are a few examples.

Boogie-Blues Six

This example piece makes use of the 'chopping' type bass-line, although it has the addition of the 7th note in some places.

This example boogie-blues employs the use of repetitive thirds throughout, starting from the very first bar (as below). The timing for this when played with the left-hand is quite simple as the first and third notes of each triplet coincide with the bass notes. Shown below is an example of this, with each triplet counted out, the right-hand matching the left-hand.

Short runs like the one below often use the blues scales, bar 11 uses the notes from the 'C' minor blues scale. Note that this bar is actually an 'F' chord, being the 'IV' chord. The scales from the 'I' chord also work over the 'IV' and 'V'.

Bar 13 sees a simple yet effective turnaround. This gives a nice aggressive pounding sound from which to launch into the next twelve bars.

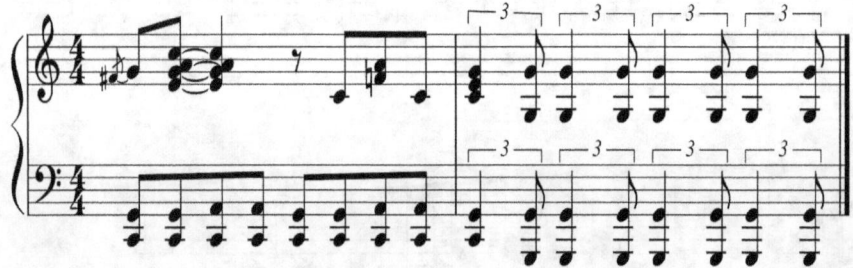

The second turnaround is a more complex two bar example that has an octave based walk up to the 5th with the left-hand. Note that in this case the same turnaround is also used for the ending. Turnarounds and endings tend to be generally interchangeable with only slight alterations. The alterations needed because an ending is moving towards the 'I' chord as opposed to the turnaround moving towards the 'V' chord.

Starting on bar 26, instead of beginning the next twelve bar sequence as usual we have a 'Break' put in place. These obviously vary but generally the left-hand goes quiet or is reduced to a few stabbing notes to re-enforce the beat, while the right-hand plays some sort of lick over the top.

The following two bars then create a build-up to continue with the piece, with the left-hand walking upwards and in this case the right-hand then creates a rhythmic counterpart over the top.

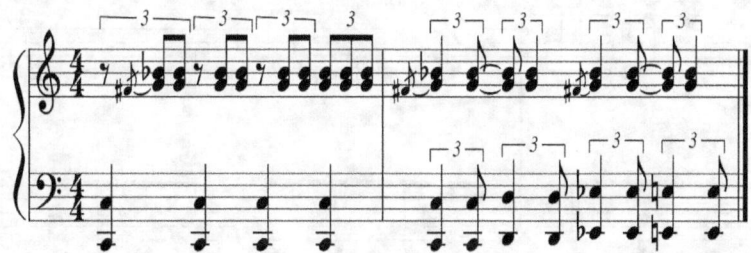

Note that this has taken up four bars in total, so looking at your twelve bar progression you will continue onwards at bar five, which is your 'IV' chord.

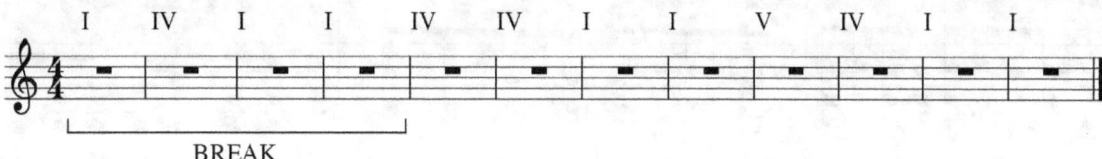

Boogie-Blues Six

Boogie-Blues seven

This next example is a very rhythmic example of a boogie-blues, this time in the key of 'A' and using a swing/shuffle feel. The left-hand is the familiar 'chop' type although this time some chord changes are set up in the previous bar. This is done by playing one semi-tone lower than the target notes of the new chord. You can of course play this without the step-up at the chord change if you prefer.

This boogie-blues also alters the chord progression slightly in places, as in bars 3 and 7 it switches from the 'I' chord to the 'IV' for half a bar. This isn't done all the time, but it does add an extra degree of interest to the piece, but could equally be played without these changes if you prefer.

The right-hand plays in a rhythmic fashion, predominantly chords that keep in line with the left-hand for most of the time.

A version of the classic blues' turnaround (shown below) with slight variations is used throughout. Changing the left-hand to quavers instead of crotchets in bar 24.

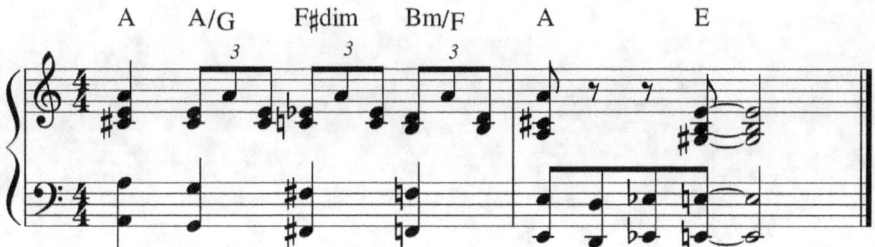

The use of drone notes can be seen on bar 38, note that here the same pattern is carried over from the 'I' chord to the 'IV' chord. On the return to the 'I' chord it has opted to change the top note, keeping the lower two the same.

The triplet sections are fairly similar being based on the minor blues scale, in this case 'A' minor blues over all three of the 'I', 'IV' and 'V' chords.

Boogie-Blues Seven

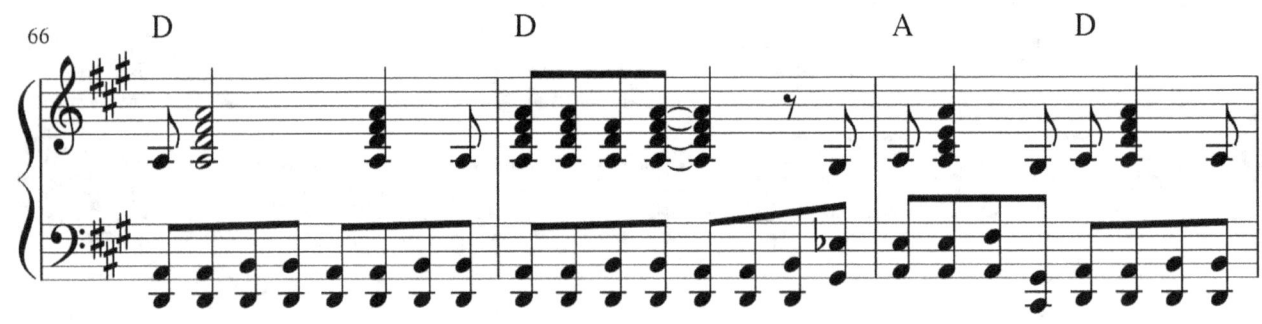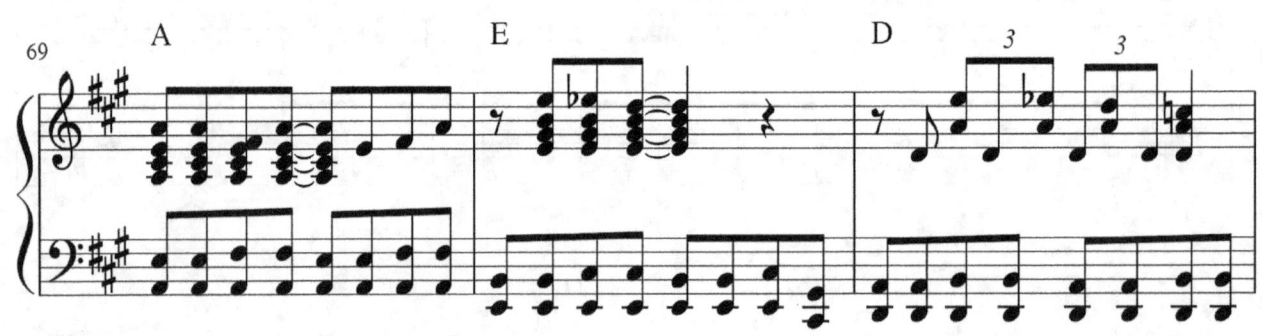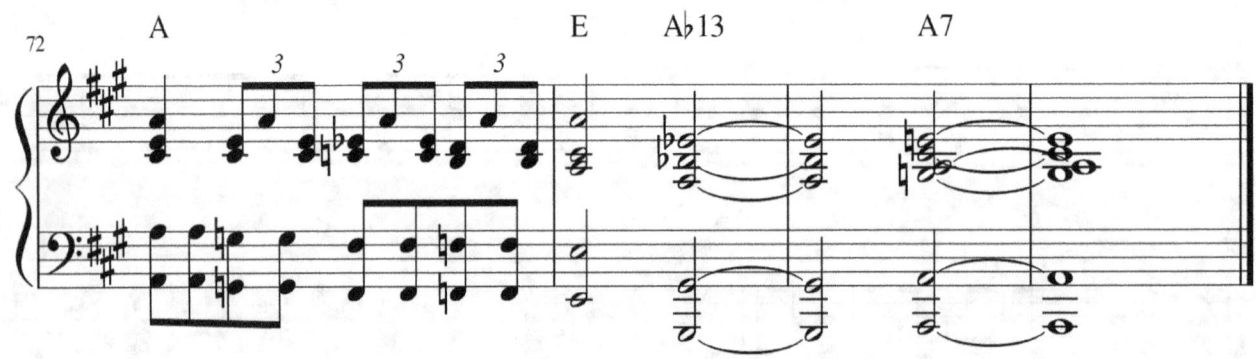

Boogie-Blues Eight

This example is intended to be slightly slower at around 100 bpm, but still using the swing/shuffle feel. The left-hand has a suspension type syncopated feel with the last note of beat four being carried over into beat one of the following bar. The bass pattern itself is the familiar boogie type, but it now contains some single notes. This gives a different feel as you are moving from the root to the higher notes (5th, 6th, 7th) creating a bass that kind of rocks back and forth.

The main right-hand riff is repeated throughout, consisting of a chord (root and 5th) and some fourth intervals which use the same notes as fifths, but in reverse order. Perhaps the chord and the third beat needs slightly emphasising here.

The syncopated pattern found on several bars has quite interesting timing and makes for a good contrast. The timing is shown in no.2, with more detail.

1.

2.

Boogie-Blues Eight

Blues One

This example uses a left-hand bass riff that gives a different more laid back feel than the more frantic boogie-blues pieces. Played slower again at around 90 bpm, in the key of 'F' with a swing/shuffle feel. Due to the timing some of this is notated as triplets to aid in its reading.

The main left-hand riff is built from the notes (1st, 5th, ♭3rd, 6th, 3rd). The first notes on the second and fourth beats are played slightly late (although emphasised and short/sharp, this is important, don't hang onto these notes) to create a laid back feel.

On both bars 30 and 31 you have a continuous roll using (in descending order) the 9th, 7th, 6th, 5th, 3rd. These might look complex but in reality they are just an arpeggiated chord that is repeated over and over again.

Starting from the fifth finger, the 7th and 6th would then be played with the third finger sliding off from one to the other, finishing with the first finger/thumb.

Blues One

Blues Two

This blues example in the key of 'C' uses dotted quavers and semi-quavers to portray the swing/shuffle feel. It uses a medium tempo with a constant rhythm from the somewhat melodic left-hand. You may have heard something similar before, I'd say it's more of a Chicago electric blues' thing, and often the entire band will follow the bass-line for a time before breaking off.

The bass-line consists of just the root/1st over two octaves, with the 7th and 5th. This same riff follows the chord changes through the entire piece.

The main right-hand riff is really a guitar based one, although it adapts to the piano quite well. It consists of two chords, a 'C6' that drops down to a rootless 'C9'.

When played, you have the option to slide the 3rd on the first chord, coming down off the minor 3rd onto the major 3rd. This adds a somewhat guitar like element to the sound (to a degree). This idea is only written into the example piece at the later stages, but use it as freely as you want.

A degree of jumping up and down the keyboard is required, as you will switch from the comping type chord riff to melodic parts an octave higher. In a band situation you might not do this quite as much, but playing solo is a different proposition, having to be all things yourself.

Blues Two

Blues Three

This medium paced example is in the key of 'C', written predominantly using triplets at around the 90 bpm mark or where-ever you feel comfortable. Although this is meant to be at a sedate/medium pace, the riff could also work at a faster tempo, but that would create a very different feel. The right-hand is kept simple which highlights the slightly more complex and melodic left-hand.

The one bar left-hand uses the 1st and 5th, moving up to the 7th and 6th and resembles the 'chopping' type boogie bass-line except the notes are mostly broken (separate) and has the added three note triplet run at the end (b3rd, 3rd, 5th). Note how the last note of the first bar is carried over into the second bar.

To help clarify the timing, below shows the riff with the triplet values added to help with counting out the timing.

The right-hand is mostly a mixture of tremolos like this.

And comping type chords patterns like this.

Blues Three

Walking-Bass

The term 'walking bass' is found in many styles of music and perhaps obviously gets its name from the way it walks up and down the scale/keyboard. Being that we are talking about a 'slow-blues', this is done in a laid back manner, rather than the more frantic walking-bass found in boogie-woogie piano.

The notes used for a walking bass are generally any sequence of notes that will work within the chord structure. The main notes from any chord are the 1st, 3rd, 5th, with the 6th and 7th being the next in importance for us here. Most other notes are useable, but generally more as passing notes or when moving to the next chord.

Main target notes for walking bass lines (Key of 'C')

1st, 3rd, 5th, 6th, 7th

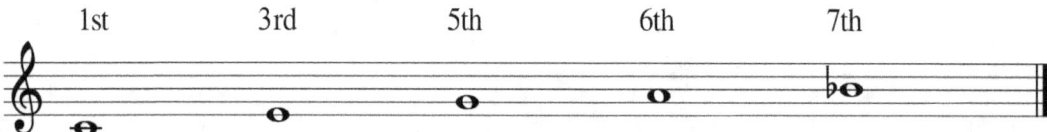

Secondary passing notes (Key of 'C')

♭9th, 9th, ♭3rd, 4th, ♭5th, ♯5th

You may have noticed the major 7th has been omitted, this is because the dominant 7th is favoured, with the major sounding out of place. It is possible to use one as a passing note at times (shown below) but even then, carefully.

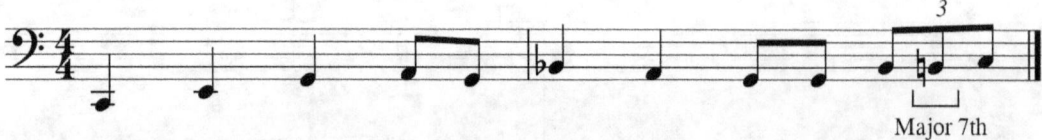

Major 7th

1.

Starting from the root/1st moving up through the 3rd, 5th, 6th to the root octave and then back down in reverse order. Although perhaps a little too 'happy' sounding.

2.

Here the bass walks up to the 7th instead of the root/1st creating more of what might be termed a 'blues' type sound.

3.

Here the last beat of bar one is split by briefly dropping back down to the 5th. (Remember that these two notes are played as triplets using a swing/shuffle feel, and not as straight quavers).

4.

This takes the first bar of the previous line and simply repeats it.

5.

From the root, jump up one octave and now walk downwards instead, this time you're also incorporating the minor third.

When it comes to changing chords, you can play around with the bass-line using different combinations of passing notes in order to move towards your destination note (that being the root of the next chord).

1.

When moving from the 'I' chord to the 'IV' chord a common trick is to walk-up almost chromatically, going from the root note of the first chord to the root of the next. Starting from the root, skip the flattened ninth and move up a semi-tone at a time until you reach the root of the 'IV' chord.

2.

You can walk the bass down towards the root note of the next chord, in this example ending two semi-tones above the destination note 'F'.

3.

An additional note in-between for a more direct connection.

4.

Or alternatively.

5.

After moving downwards you step back up towards the root of the following 'IV' chord, the 'F'.

6.

You don't always have to be directly/physically next to the destination note, here once you are one semi-tone below the 'F' you jump down one octave for the root of the next chord.

7.

Or use the next note of the 'IV' chord as normal.

With the option of then walking back downwards (option 1) or moving upwards again (option 2) and so into to the next octave range.

Option 1

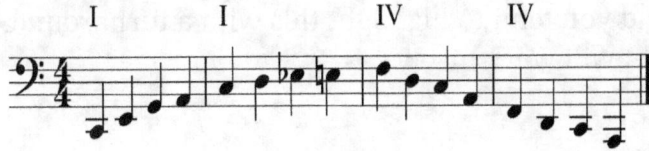

Option 2

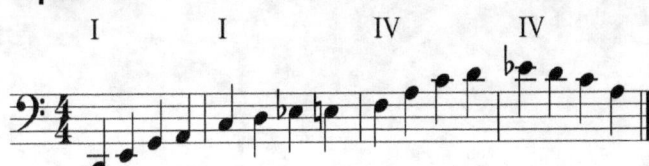

8.

When moving from the 'I' chord to the 'V' chord you could walk down towards the chords root (here a 'G') by using the three semi-tones above the destination note, moving chromatically through them.

9.

Alternatively, end on the destination note 'G' at the end of the preceding bar, but then drop down an octave for the actual chord change.

10.

Or introduce some triplets for a faster run up towards the new chord.

11.

Moving from the last 'I' chord of a twelve bar sequence to the first 'I' chord of the next is similar to a chord change, and you tend to highlight this with a turnaround. This is a simple walking bass lick that will work nicely.

Thirty-six bars of how some of these bass-line riffs might work together. It is a good idea to practice the walking-bass separately to begin with, as it needs to be fairy well ingrained in your subconscious to have left/right-hand independence.

Jumping-Blues

This example uses a walking-bass line throughout, with the first twelve-bar chorus using a strong on-off rhythm. The bass being played on the beat with the chord being off the beat.

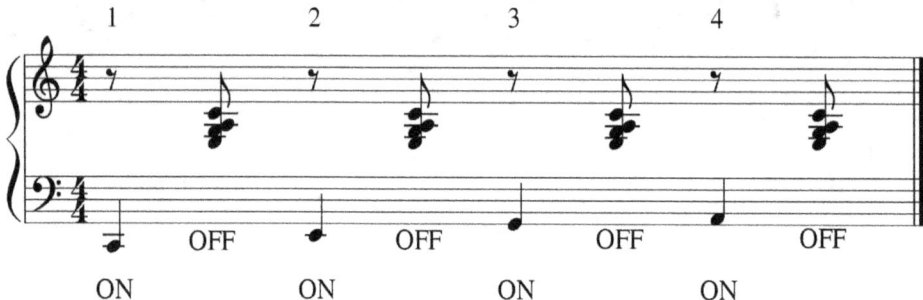

This is using a chord progression that alters bars 9 and 10 compared to a standard twelve bar progression. Bar 9 uses the 'II' chord, with bar 10 now being the 'V' chord. Also note that the 'II' chord is a minor chord (in this case 'Dm').

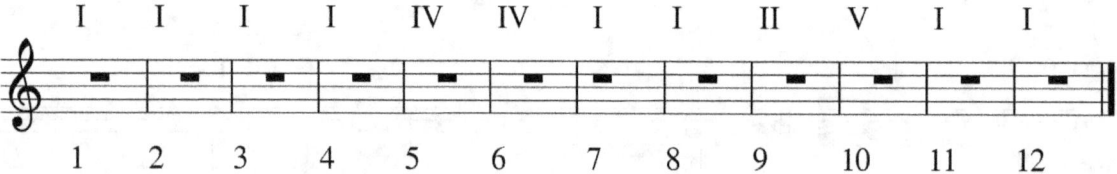

The piece has been written using single notes with the left-hand, but you could change this for octaves or even use the more 'boogie' type alternating octave left-hand instead, or even change between them as you play.

Jumping-Blues

Slow-Blues

A slow blues, is obviously played at a slower pace, perhaps around 80bpm might be typical, but it's not only the tempo that creates the slower feel but the left-hand bass-line, being far more sedate than the boogie-blues type riffs. I will point out that although a 'slow blues' is generally slower in bpm and feel, it is not always slow to play, you will often hear or play some very fast passages with the right-hand. I'm sure you've heard guitarists soloing at three million miles an hour over a slow piece, trying to fill every space. Well you can do the same with the piano, although it is best not to go over board, keep it musical.

When it comes to slow-blues on the piano there are various left-hands you can employ, from walking type bass-lines, stride type piano and even boogie-type riffs that have been slowed down, but we will start with the walking-bass.

Slow-Blues-Walking

This next slow-blues uses the same type of walking bass-line that has been covered over the last few pages. The right-hand starts off with some simple fairly sparse chords, just comping over the top of the bass-line for the first couple of twelve bar sequences, nothing overly fancy.

Dropping the chords down by one semi-tone, moving from a major chord to a diminished chord works well on the chord changes.

Once the blues has been warmed into, the later stages then become more aggressive with the use of triplet patterns and cross-over type licks.

Slow-Blues Walking

Slow-Blues - Eight-Bar

Here we are changing from the more common twelve-bar format to the eight-bar. Although this doesn't really alter the content of a blues, it feels quite different to play as each eight bar sequence comes round far quicker than with the twelve bar. This does have a shuffle feel, although this time it has been written with both dotted quavers and semi-quavers and actual triplets.

There are various chord progressions for an eight-bar blues, but here we are using a relatively simple version with only bar seven complicating things with its own chord change.

The bass-line used can also be heard in boogie-woogie although perhaps at a slightly faster pace, but it slows down nicely to work well within a slow piece. It consists of the root note at octaves, with the 3rd and the 5th. There are two variations of this bass-line used here.

1.   **2.**

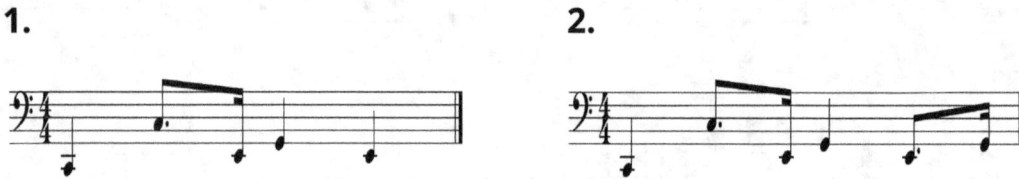

The turnaround to this employs a little bit of 'stride' piano on each seventh bar of the eight bar progression. Stride piano uses a low bass note and then a chord higher up the keyboard. Here we are just using a 'C' major chord and then the 'F7'.

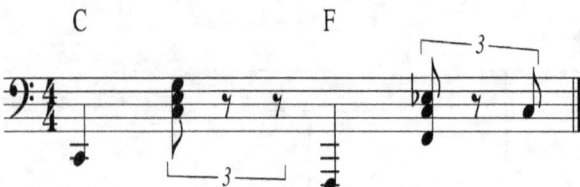

Slow-Blues – Eight-Bar

Eight-Bar In 12/8

12/8 Timing Signature

When music in 4/4 timing is constructed predominantly with triplets, it can instead be notated in 12/8. Referred to as such because it uses eighth notes (hence the 8) with twelve eighth notes per bar (hence the 12). If you take the twelve eighth notes and divide them by four (four beats per bar in 4/4) you get three, which is the equivalent to a set of triplets in 4/4. The resulting music is exactly the same, but it saves the need for having triplet signs clouding the music.

4/4 timing with triplets (Four beats per bar, each divided by three).

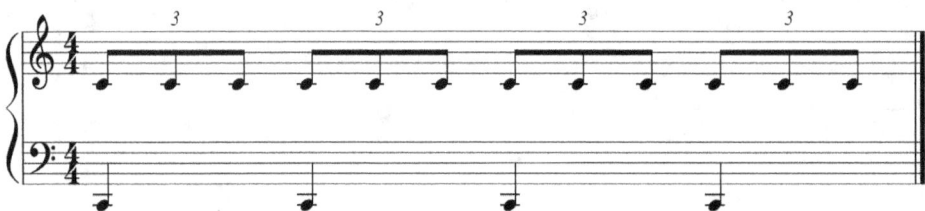

12/8 timing. Each group of three eighth notes is the equivalent to a set of triplets in the 4/4 timing above, but now with no need for the triplet signs.

The following blues example piece uses the common bass pattern shown below, with a triplet feel right-hand accompaniment for the first eight bars and then varying it for the second eight.

Eight-Bar 12/8

Slow-Blues Stride

Stride

The term 'stride' can be a confusing one, as it is both a style of music and a style of playing that's used in several styles of music. 'Harlem stride piano' is a jazz style that sprang up during the 1920s – 1930s, it is claimed to have developed from Ragtime, although the two have many differences, for one thing it was more of a improvisational style whereas Ragtime was very much composed, indeed, Scott Joplin is said to have considered it to be classical music at the time. The confusion comes with them both using a bass note on the first and third beats, with a chord on the second and fourth beats, resulting in the player striding up and down the keyboard. Actual 'stride' piano tended to be a faster more improvisational style with greater distances often being used with the left-hand. While Harlem stride piano is a style to itself, the style of playing lends itself to other styles of music. As already mentioned, ragtime uses a similar form, and this can also be carried over into the blues, fortunately at a slower pace.

The basic 'stride' style in the key of 'C'. A bass note is followed by a chord on alternate beats of the bar. Beat one is a bass note with beat two being a chord, this is then repeated again and again.

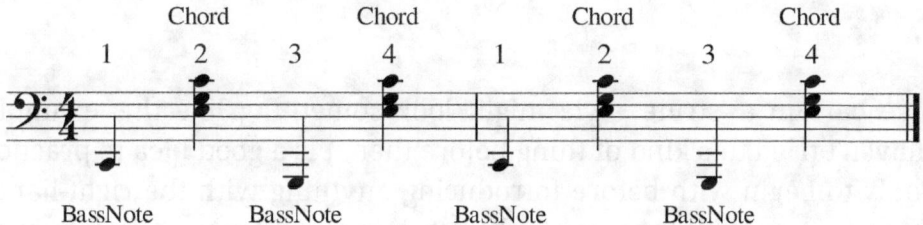

Note how 'stride' varies the bass note, switching between the root note 'C' and the fifth 'G'. In a very slow blues piano piece you can sometimes use the root note again without sounding too repetitive.

1. Root and fifth

2. Root repeated

Chords can of course be played in different positions and this applies when playing in a 'stride' style. Altering the inversion creates a slightly different sound, although the root position is probably the most common.

Root Position

First Inversion

Second Inversion

A typical twelve bars in a 'stride' style might look something like this example below. If you haven't tried this kind of thing before then it is a good idea to practice the left-hand only to begin with before introducing anything with the right-hand, being very important to build up left/right-hand independence. The constant leaping from one end to another may seem strange at first, but will become second nature with time and practice.

When approaching chord changes you can break up the 'stride' with a few walking/step-up notes at the end of the first chord, these lead into the next chord. Examples below in the key of 'C' show a few possibilities.

In the second bar on the last beat, instead of another chord we have the 3rd which is just one semi-tone below the destination chords root note (being an 'F').

Instead of the chord in the second bar we have a short chromatic run upwards, using the 9th, ♭3rd and 3rd, ending on the 3rd just below the destination note.

On the last two beats of bar two we move downwards using the 5th and ♭5th (octaves being optional) this time finishing one semi-tone above the destination chord root note (being an 'F').

The same idea also applies when changing from the 'I' chord to the 'V' chord. Finishing one-semi-tone below the destination note (now a 'G') using the 4th and ♭5th of the 'I' chord.

Slow-Blues Stride One

The following example in the key of 'C' should be played at around 75-85 bpm with a swing/shuffle feel, using a simple 'stride' type left-hand. The left-hand changes in places between using only the root and using the 5th for the bass note.

The chord progression varies on bars three and seven, switching to the 'IV' chord for the second half of the bars.

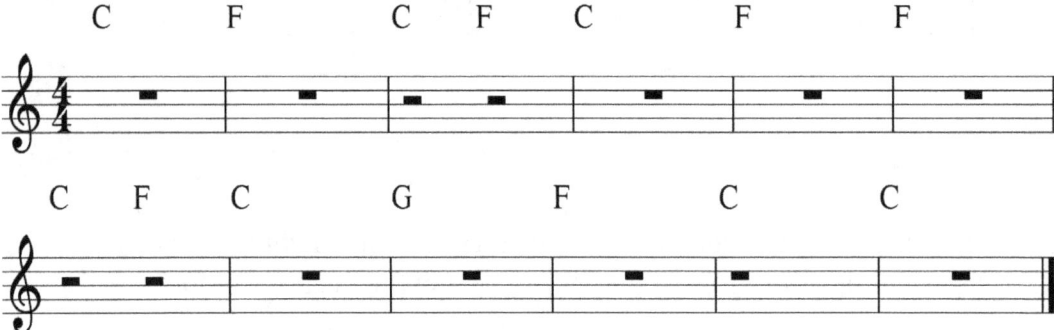

The same chord progression shown as Roman numerals.

Slow-Blues Stride One

Slow-Blues Stride Two

This is a slight departure in that it is a minor blues, with all chords being played being of the minor variety. Written in the key of 'G' and to be played around the 60 bpm mark. This is notated predominantly using triplets to allow for easier understanding of the timing.

The twelve bar chord progression varies slightly from standard merely with the extra changes in bars 3,7 and 11, where it switches to the 'IV' chord for half the bar.

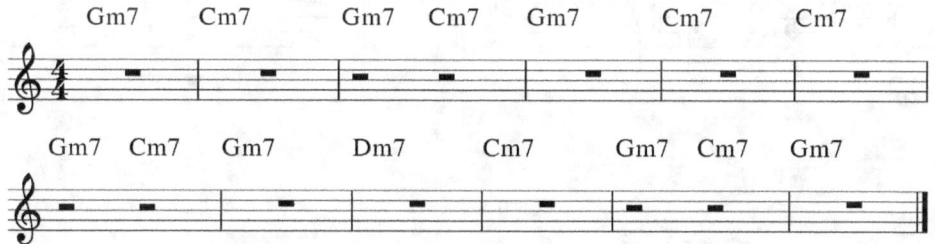

Chord progression shown as Roman numerals.

Being a slow blues, it switches between two kinds of right-hand playing, from slow comping type chord work (1) to faster right-hand passages over the slow and steady left-hand (2).

1.   **2.**

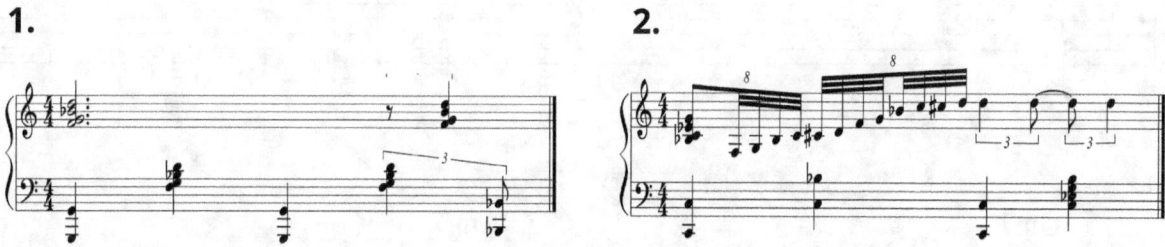

The slower the blues piece is, the more feel that is required to be put into the playing. Play this as expressively as possible, from slow and gentle to fast and aggressive, blues music switches between them at a moments notice. The best way to learn how to play with feeling is simply to listen to as much music as you can, only by doing this can you internalise the sound and so be armed with the knowledge to reproduce it.

Slow-Blues Stride Two

Slow-Blues Stride/Tenths

The main point of interest of the next 'stride based blues is its use of tenths in the left-hand. A tenth interval creates a great sounding harmony, but only if you can reach them. People aren't physically all the same, so not everyone is able to stretch their left-hand to span a tenth interval. But don't worry if you can't, as there are ways around this for people with smaller hands.

The 10th is found by counting up ten degrees through the major scale. The example below (key of 'C') shows that the root is 'C' and the 10th is 'E'. You will notice that this note is the same as the 3rd degree, but it is called a 10th when it is counted further up the scale. The ten degrees spacing between these two notes creates the interval referred to as a tenth. You may or may not be-able to stretch your hand to playing the 'C' and 'E' together, although the key of 'C' is easier than some other keys for this.

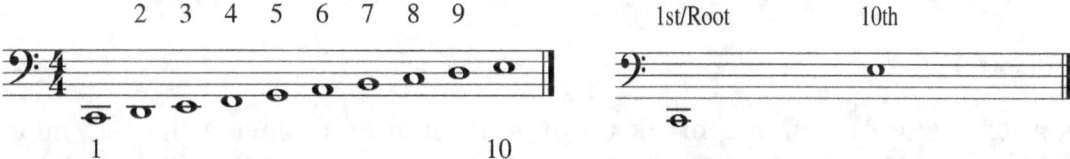

Within 'stride' you are playing tenths for the first and third beats instead of single notes or octaves, with the chord played on the second and fourth beats as usual.

If you move down to the 5th on beat three, you can no longer use a tenth as the tenth interval formed from this point is no-longer relevant to the chord you are on.

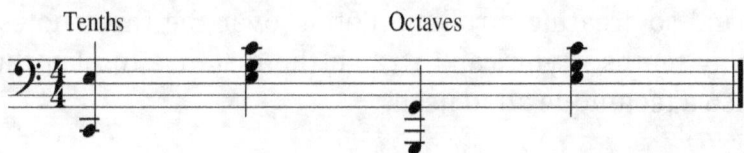

It is also possible to add an extra harmony note in-between with your index finger, like the 5th or the dominant 7th, although personally I feel this can sound a little muddy, but the 5th can certainly work at times.

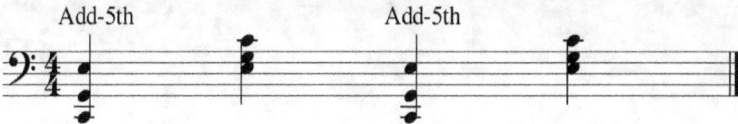

There are three ways to play a tenth interval with the left-hand, some make the use of tenths possible for those of us with slighter smaller hands.

1. Simultaneously
2. Broken
3. Rolling

1. Simultaneously

Simultaneously we have already covered. As the word suggests, this is when you play the root and tenth at the same time, potentially quite challenging.

2. Broken

Broken tenths are when you break the interval into two, playing the two notes separately. Play the root note first with your little finger (5) and then (releasing the key) play the 10th with your thumb (1). This isn't ONLY for people with smaller hands, this technique has a charm and sound all of its own.

Two possible ways of timing this, holding the two bass notes with the sustain pedal.

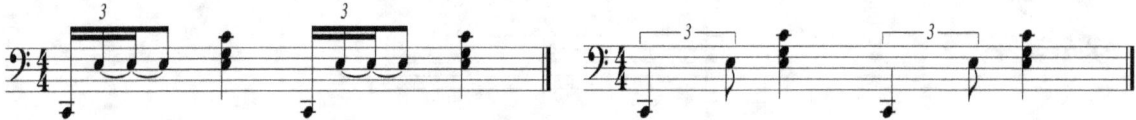

3. Rolling

For this you need to include an extra note in-between the 1st and 10th playing them in series, lowest note first, and so creating a rolling motion over the three notes. Although this is a way to play tenths if you can't stretch the distance to play the notes simultaneously, it is also a technique all to itself.

Hold the sustain pedal to create the effect of the 10th harmony.

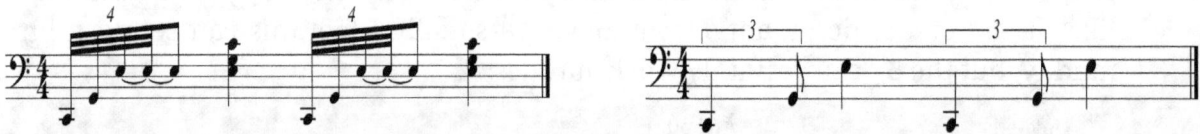

This 'stride' based blues has a slight nod towards a New Orleans feel, written in the key of 'G' and played at around the 70bpm mark with a swing/shuffle feel using tenths in the left-hand throughout. Some are written to be played simultaneously, but if this doesn't work for you then you can create a similar effect by playing them in a broken fashion, holding one note with the sustain pedal as you move to play the second note of the interval.

The left-hand contains a short run up to the 10th in places. Note how the 10th is actually played first with the root being brought in just after while the 10th is held. You can release the tenth holding it with the sustain pedal while you move down to the root if need be.

This alternative way of playing this kind of riff contains an extra note in the run.

To keep the left-hand interesting the second bass note in the bar is replaced by this syncopated addition. Using the 5th and ♭3rd with the ♭3rd quickly moving up to the 3rd on the third beat.

Slow-Blues Stride/Tenths

New Orleans Rhythms

The New Orleans style of blues piano has a different feel to it than any other form of blues. It is heavily influenced by strong Caribbean rhythms (like the Tango and Rumba) and is quite heavily syncopated. Below are a few variations on the rhythm in question, get used to just playing the rhythm to begin with.

1.

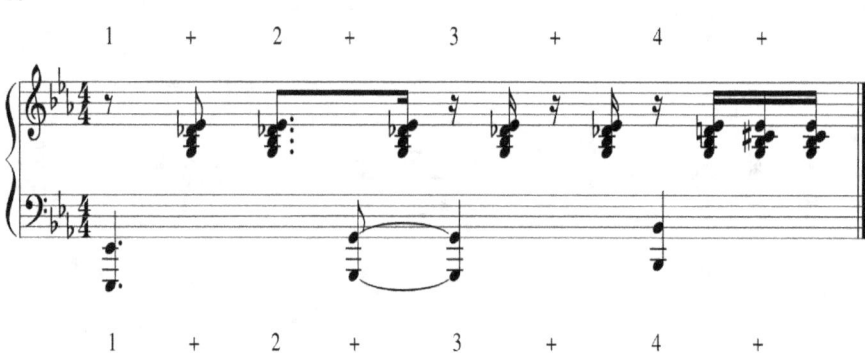

2.

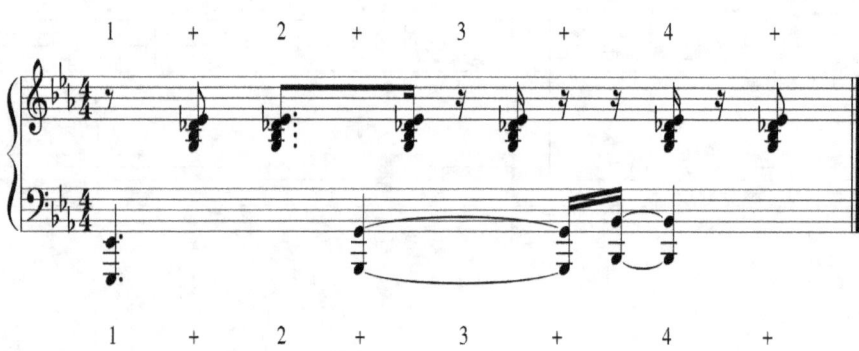

3.

New Orleans Rumba

New Orleans Style One

This New Orleans inspired example uses a strong Rumba type rhythm in the left-hand. Written in the key of 'C' and to be played roughly around 110-120 bpm.

The left-hand being used here uses the root/1st, 3rd and 5th. It is written here as single notes, but it can also be played as octaves for a larger sound.

Another common feature of New Orleans piano is the use of drummer type 'ruffs', for want of a better word and description. Playing a very fast group of notes that lead up to the target note.

These can be three notes, two or even one as in the simplified version used on the bass-line below. The last note of the bar uses a grace note, going from the ♭5th to the 5th very quickly, just before the first beat of the next bar (in this case sliding from one to the other with the same finger).

Another common feature is the use of an arpeggiated chord where the notes are held when played until a full chord is produced.

Another aspect of the style is the way it often sets up the 'I' to 'IV' chord changes with turnarounds that are unique to New Orleans piano.

1.

2.

3.

4.

New Orleans Style One

New Orleans Bass-Lines

Alternative New Orleans Bass-Lines

1.

2.

3.

4.

5.

6.

New Orleans Style Two

The next example piece uses a few variations of the same left-hand.

A type of riff found in New Orleans music unusually makes use of the major seventh chord. This is used in a transitional movement to the dominant seventh.

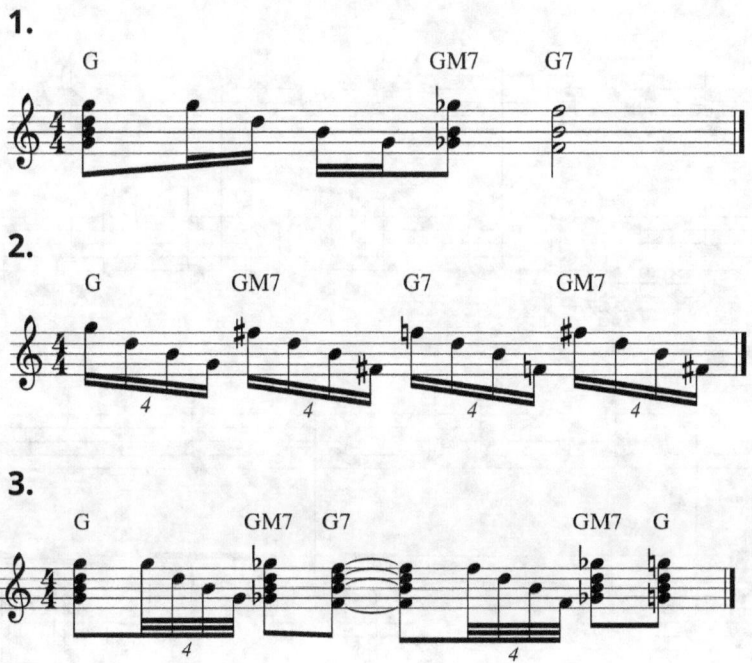

New Orleans Style Two

Practice Ideas

Practice Time

It stands to reason that to make progress in anything in life you have to spend time doing it. The piano is no different, so pointing out the obvious, the more time you spend practising the quicker you will progress. That said, in reality not everyone has all the time in the world so use your time carefully. You may think you haven't got the time to spend on it but stop and think about it for a moment. If you break down and analyse how you spend your day, most people can find or make a little time, even if its only ten or twenty minutes here and there, it all adds up.

Consistency wins the day in most things, and practising the piano is something that should be done with consistency. This keeps it fresh in your mind, which makes a world of difference compared to practising in fits and starts with days and days in-between. If you want to improve, practice as regularly as possible.

While huge marathon practice sessions at the weekend might be fine, it is extremely beneficial to have regular (even if shorter) practice sessions every day, or maybe even several in one day as these don't have to be long. Ten, twenty or thirty minutes practice sessions on a regular basis are worth their weight in gold, and really... this isn't a massive amount of time to take out of your day.

Left / Right-Hand Independence

Piano blues music (in all its various forms) requires a certain degree of left and right-hand independence. Therefore, it is highly recommended that you practice these separately, at least initially until you feel you are comfortable with them. Ideally you want to get to the point where you can play a twelve-bar blues left-hand while partially concentrating on something else. A common one to try is to watch the television while you practice the left-hand, or even reading a book. Another trick is to try playing with your eyes closed as this requires you to go very much by feel and your memory of the physical patterns/movements that are made. Both are very good techniques to see where you are at, if not for general practise.

Metronome

It is a good idea to practice using a metronome at times (although not always) as this will help improve your timing. If you practice without and then turn one on you can find out if you're lagging in places, or even in-front of the timing sometimes, so this is a good thing to help keep your timing tight. If you can, even set up a suitable blues drum backing track or even play along to an actual recording (although not as good for highlighting your own mistakes, it is a good way to get the feel of the music down).

Tempo

Whatever you are working on, when you first start out practice at a slow tempo. If you can't play it slow perfectly then you certainly can't play it fast. And playing too fast will only introduce mistakes, and you really don't want to keep making the same mistakes. When you continuously play the same mistake over and over again you are learning that mistake, even if you know it is a mistake your brain is getting used to doing it. So if there is a difficult part you can't master, slow it down until you can play it perfectly at the slower speed. Once you have mastered it at the slower tempo gradually increase it until you are back at the full speed of the piece.

Different Keys

Although many examples in this book are based in the key of 'C' (for ease of learning, as 'C' is a lovely key for the piano) make sure you take anything you learn and transpose them into other keys. F and G are probably the two next most common ones on the piano, although there are obviously many more. One technique for doing this is to take a new riff that you have learnt and practice it around the circle of fifths. This is a great way to hit every key, although admittedly quite time-consuming it will make a massive difference to you in the long run.

Listening To Music

Whatever style of music you are practicing it is important to listen to it on regular basis. When you listen to the music you will gradually absorb the sound and the feel of it which will then enable you to reproduce it. This is an extremely important point, as think about it, if you had never heard a single blues song in your life, do you really think you would be able to learn and play it? Simple answer is no, as you'd have no idea of the feeling the music creates, so this is a vital part of learning a style of music, so keep listening as much as possible.

Downloadable Audio

Audio files based on the examples within the book are available to download from the website in MP3 format, simply follow the instructions below.

To access and download the MP3 audio files, simply visit the website...

www.tylermusic.co.uk

- Click on audio downloads
- Select the relevant book title
- Enter the password... **complete831**
- Click on the download icon

Once downloaded please save them for future use.

Index

Introduction	1	Rolls	110 - 115
Blues Styles	3 - 6	Drone Notes	116 - 117
Major Scales	9 - 13	Cluster Notes	118
Roman Numerals	14 - 15	Boogie-Blues	121 - 124
12-Bar Chord Progressions	16 - 21	Boogie-Blues.1	125 - 128
8-Bar Chord Progressions	22 - 23	Boogie-Blues.2	129 - 131
16-Bar Chord Progressions	24	Boogie-Blues.3	132 - 134
Fingering Numbering	25	Boogie-Blues.4	135 - 137
Blues Shuffle Feel	26 - 27	Boogie-Blues.5	138 - 145
Chords Triads	28	Turnarounds	146 - 148
Chords Sixths	29	Cross-Over Licks	149
Chords Sevenths	30 - 31	Boogie-Blues.6	150 - 154
Chords Ninths	32 - 36	Boogie-Blues.7	155 - 162
Chords Thirteenths	37 - 40	Boogie-Blues.8	163 - 167
Rootless Chord Voicings	41 - 44	Blues.1	168 - 172
Scales For Blues	45	Blues.2	173 - 176
Major Pentatonic Scales	46 - 50	Blues.3	177 - 179
Major Blues Scales	51 - 55	Walking Bass	180 - 185
Using Major Scales	56 - 59	Jumping Blues	186 - 189
Minor Pentatonic Scales	60 - 64	Slow Blues - Walking	190 - 193
Minor Blues Scales	65 - 69	Slow Blues 8-Bar	194 - 197
Using Minor Scales	70 - 73	12/8 Timing 8-Bar	198 - 200
Relative Scales	74 - 76	Stride Piano	201 - 203
Scale Practice	77 - 78	Slow Blues Stride.1	204 - 206
Combining Scales	79 - 80	Slow Blues Stride.2	207 - 210
Mixolydian Mode	81 - 87	Stride With Tenths	211 - 213
Mixolydian Triads	88 - 89	Slow Blues Stride.3 10ths	214 - 217
Third Intervals	90 - 96	New Orleans Rhythm	218 - 220
Sixth Intervals	97 - 99	New Orleans.1	221 - 225
3 – 7 Intervals	100	New Orleans Bass-Lines	226
Grace Notes	101 - 103	New Orleans.2	227 - 230
Tremolos	104 - 108	Practicing Ideas	231 - 232
Arpeggios	109	Downloadable Audio	233

Want to learn more blues piano...

Other great titles to take you further

Piano Blues Scales

The ultimate guide to learning the blues scales for the piano. The scales are clearly shown and explained in all keys for both major and minor scales along with fingering suggestions. But it doesn't stop there, here we go further and include ideas like the combined scales and methods of how to practice and use the scales in a more musical and practical real world fashion.

Easy New-Orleans

Easy New Orleans will take you on a journey into the wonderful world of New-Orleans piano. Take your first steps into this unique style, the music of Legends such as Professor Long Hair, Dr John and James Booker. From beginners well into intermediate, it covers the basics with easy to understand clear explanations with example pieces throughout that start off easy and gradually increase in difficulty, while adding extra elements along the way. With downloadable audio available

Blues Piano (Specifics Series)

The series that concentrates on specific aspects of blues piano. The first volume concentrating on the left-hand, looking in detail at the walking-bass. What is it? how's it created? And how do you about playing it in the blues environment? Other titles look at the stride style of playing and then concentrating on the right hand.

Start playing authentic blues today

Tyler music.co.uk

For further piano books (including spiral bound editions)
sheet music and information on blues
and boogie woogie music
visit the website at…

www.tylermusic.co.uk

**Follow us on Facebook for updates
and information on latest releases.**

Also Available

Improvising Boogie-Woogie Vol. One

Learn to play boogie-woogie like the best of them. If you want to play boogie like Albert Ammons, Axel Zwingenberger or Jools Holland then this is the series for you. The first volume in a series of books to teach boogie-woogie piano, from the basics to more advanced techniques and everything in-between, this will give you the help and material you need.

Improvising Boogie-Woogie Vol. Two

The ultimate guide to playing boogie-woogie continues with volume-two, adding more left-hand patterns and right-hand riffs, including aspects like the walking-bass pattern, a little stride, rolling chords, using tenths and more complex rhythmic ideas.

Improvising Boogie-Woogie Vol. Three

The ultimate guide to playing boogie-woogie continues with volume-three, adding even more left-hand patterns and right-hand riffs to the series. Looking at the use of thirds and sixths, the use of scaler other chord progressions how such riffs are created and how to begin to create your own.

Improvising Boogie-Woogie: The Complete Edition

All three volumes in one edition. Available as perfect bound and spiral bound (spiral available through the website only). Learn to play boogie-woogie like the best of them. If you want to play boogie like Albert Ammons, Axel Zwingenberger or Jools Holland then this is the series for you. From the basics to more advanced techniques and everything in-between.

Easy Boogie-Woogie Vol.1   For Beginners

Easy boogie-woogie takes the beginning boogie pianist through their first steps into the timeless style. It covers the basics with easy to understand clear explanations and includes example pieces throughout that start off easy and gradually increase in difficulty while adding extra elements. With downloadable audio, why not start learning boogie-woogie today.

Easy Boogie-Woogie Vol.2

This second volume of Easy Boogie-Woogie follows on from the first one, taking the beginning boogie player a step further again. New ideas and concepts are introduced along with many examples and explanations throughout. Bigger and better than ever. With downloadable audio to help you along, it's the perfect way to continue your boogie-woogie journey.

Easy Blues Piano   For Beginners

Learn to play the blues with this beginners guide for the piano. It covers the very basics of the blues, introducing the various elements that create the twelve-bar blues sound. It starts off easy, so even a relative beginner can dive in, and gradually introduces new ideas. With downloadable audio, why not start learning blues today.

Easy New-Orleans   For Beginners

Learn to play that unique style of blues piano from New Orleans, the style of Dr John, Professor Longhair and James Booker to name but a few. Covering everything from chord progressions and left-hand bass patterns and introducing the all important New-Orleans rhythm.

Piano Blues Scales

The ultimate guide to learning the blues scales for the piano. The scales are clearly shown and explained in all keys for both major and minor scales along with fingering suggestions. But it doesn't stop there, here we go further and include ideas like the combined scales and methods of how to practice and use the scales in a more musical and practical real world fashion.

Bite Sized Specifics – Blues Piano/Walking-Bass

Learn to play the walking-bass for blues piano with the first in a series that concentrates on specific aspects of blues piano. Concentrating on the left-hand, it looks at what the walking-bass is, how it is created and various ways to which you can employ it in a blues environment.

Bite Sized Specifics – Blues Piano/Stride-Piano

Learn to play blues piano using the left-hand stride style. The second in a series that concentrates on a specific aspect of blues piano. Concentrating on the left-hand, it looks at what stride is and how it is created and various ways to which you can employ it in a blues environment.

Bite Sized Specifics – Blues Piano/Right-Hand Vol.1

Learn to play blues piano with the third in a series that concentrates on specific aspects of blues piano. Concentrating on the right-hand, it concentrates on the important aspect of comping, which is the more rhythmic side of blues with an emphasis on the important use of chords and repetitive patterns/riffs that form the backbone of the music.

Tyler Music – Blues & Boogie-Woogie Piano